ANCIENTS AND MODERNS

General Editor: Phiroze Vasunia, Reader in Classics, University of Reading

How can antiquity illuminate critical issues in the modern world? How does the ancient world help us address contemporary problems and issues? In what ways do modern insights and theories shed new light on the interpretation of ancient texts, monuments, artefacts and cultures? The central aim of this exciting new series is to show how antiquity is relevant to life today. The series also points towards the ways in which the modern and ancient worlds are mutually connected and interrelated. Lively, engaging, and historically informed, *Ancients and Moderns* examines key ideas and practices in context. It shows how societies and cultures have been shaped by ideas and debates that recur. With a strong appeal to students and teachers in a variety of disciplines, including classics and ancient history, each book is written for non-specialists in a clear and accessible manner.

MARIO ERASMO is Professor of Classics at the University of Georgia. He is the author of *Reading Death in Ancient Rome* (2008), *Roman Tragedy: Theatre to Theatricality* (2004) and *Archaic Latin Verse* (2001).

ANCIENTS AND MODERNS SERIES

ANCIENTS AND MODERNS

DEATH
ANTIQVITY AND ITS LEGACY

MARIO ERASMO

OXFORD
UNIVERSITY PRESS

OXFORD
UNIVERSITY PRESS

Oxford University Press, Inc., publishes works that further Oxford University's objective of
excellence in research, scholarship, and education.

Oxford   New York
Auckland   Cape Town   Dar es Salaam   Hong Kong   Karachi
Kuala Lumpur   Madrid   Melbourne   Mexico City   Nairobi
New Delhi   Shanghai   Taipei   Toronto

With offices in
Argentina   Austria   Brazil   Chile   Czech Republic   France   Greece
Guatemala   Hungary   Italy   Japan   Poland   Portugal   Singapore
South Korea   Switzerland   Thailand   Turkey   Ukraine   Vietnam

First published by I.B.Tauris & Co. Ltd. in the United Kingdom

Published by Oxford University Press, Inc.
198 Madison Avenue, New York, New York 10016

www.oup.com

Oxford is a registered trademark of Oxford University Press

Library of Congress Cataloging-in-Publication Data

Erasmo, Mario.
Death : antiquity and its legacy / Mario Erasmo.
p. cm. — (Ancients and moderns)
Includes bibliographical references and index.
ISBN 978-0-19-538097-2 (hardcover : alk. paper) — ISBN 978-0-19-538098-9 (pbk. : alk.
paper) 1. Funeral rites and ceremonies—Greece—History. 2. Funeral rites and ceremonies—
Italy—Rome—History. 3. Greece—Social life and customs. 4. Rome (Italy)--Social life and
customs. I. Title.
GT3251.A2E73 2012
393—dc23   2011031147

ISBN (HB): 978-0-19-538097-2
ISBN (PB): 978-0-19-538098-9

Typeset in Garamond Pro by Ellipsis Digital Limited, Glasgow
Printed and bound in Great Britain by CPI Group (UK) Ltd, Croydon, CR0 4YY

CONTENTS

ACKNOWLEDGEMENTS

I continue to benefit from the interdisciplinary focus of the Centre for Death and Society (CDAS) at the University of Bath and its affiliated journal *Mortality* and the International Conference on the Social Context of Death, Dying and Disposal sponsored by the International Association for the Study of Death and Society (ASDS). I am grateful for the support of the *Ancients and Moderns* series editor Phiroze Vasunia, I.B.Tauris Executive Editor Alex Wright and editorial staff members. The scope of this book required extensive research and travel and I owe special thanks to the following in the UK, Europe, Canada and the US for their invaluable assistance and encouragement: Joel Allen, Filippo Amisano, Jim Cothran, Maureen and Michael Davies, Penelope Davies, Phillip Dunn, Dora Erasmo, Anne Glass, Shawn Harrison, Mike Jones, Josh Koons, Amy Medlock, Robert A. Pratt, Rodney Morrison, Laurie Thomas, Eric Varner, and Stewart Wadden. I am grateful to Carmen Vilalta for her generous hospitality during my research visit to Genoa. The late Victor Mallet whose brilliant career was cut short gave me an early appreciation of life in death.

FOREWORD

Ancients and Moderns comes to fruition at a propitious moment: 'reception studies' is flourishing, and the scholarship that has arisen around it is lively, rigorous, and historically informed; it makes us rethink our own understanding of the relationship between past and present. *Ancients and Moderns* aims to communicate to students and general readers the depth, energy, and excitement of the best work in the field. It seeks to engage, provoke, and stimulate, and to show how, for large parts of the world, Greco–Roman antiquity continues to be relevant to debates in culture, politics, and society.

The series does not merely accept notions such as 'reception' or 'tradition' without question; rather, it treats these concepts as contested categories and calls into question the illusion of an unmediated approach to the ancient world. We have encouraged our authors to take intellectual risks in the development of their ideas. By challenging the assumption of a direct line of continuity between antiquity and modernity, these books explore how discussions in such areas as gender, politics, race, sex, and slavery occur within particular contexts and histories; they demonstrate that no culture is monolithic, that claims to ownership of the past are never pure, and that East and West are often connected together in ways that continue to surprise and disturb many. Thus, *Ancients and Moderns* is intended to stir up debates about and within reception studies and to complicate some of the standard narratives about the 'legacy' of Greece and Rome.

All the books in *Ancients and Moderns* illustrate that *how* we think about the past bears a necessary relation to *who* we are in the present. At the same time, the series also seeks to persuade scholars of antiquity that their own pursuit is inextricably connected to what many generations have thought, said, and done about the ancient world.

Phiroze Vasunia

PREFACE

The invitation to write this book arrived on the day of my mother's funeral. I could not pass on the symbolism of the timing. Events earlier in the day had already made me realize that funerals, however basic the elements surrounding mourning and burial, contained the potential for vastly different rites and interpretations depending on one's personal experience and knowledge of diverse cultures. If subject to interpretation, then they are also subject to misinterpretation with unexpected consequences.

At my mother's burial service, the casket was placed on a mechanical device that would lower it into the ground. Family members, relatives and friends were invited to take a rose from the casket spray thinking that they would toss it into the ground once the casket was lowered. The casket, however, was lowered only a foot to serve, I realized, as a symbolic burial before the actual burial that would take place after everyone left the cemetery. When the funeral director announced that the burial service was over, we were confused, still holding roses, and asked if the casket could be lowered completely. The mechanical device was not set up for a full lowering but he managed to lower the casket another foot and then announced for a second time that the burial service was over. Rather than throw roses into the ground, they were placed back into the casket spray. There was a sense that the burial service was incomplete and when leaving the cemetery, I wondered whether a symbolic burial was a burial. Did I just symbolically bury my mother?

On a follow up visit to the cemetery, the cemetery director who had spoken with the funeral director apologized for not asking whether we had wanted a full lowering of the casket at the burial service. She explained that she thought a full lowering of caskets was only done at Chinese funerals. Due to our own assumptions of what constituted a burial we did not specify a full lowering of the casket – if a burial is the placing of a body into the ground, does a burial service not mean the placing of a body into the ground when family members are present? Or is the purpose of a burial service the leave taking of the deceased at the place of burial with the actual burial occurring sometime following the service? There is no right way to bury someone, of course, and experiencing the circumstances of my mother's burial allowed me to question the subjectivity inherent in one's expectations, interpretation, and practice of traditional funerary rituals. These experiences also allowed me to frame modern funerary practices in relation to ancient rituals more than the thesis of my *Reading Death in Ancient Rome* book allowed for which I used my father's successive tombstones as inspiration and starting point to take a semiotic approach to archaeological and literary evidence.

Traditional rites and commemoration, at once solemn and vibrant, have shaped modern rites and practices that are becoming less sombre and increasingly unique with theme funerals, cremation displays, memorial tattoos, and virtual memorials. The paradox of the dead as undead is evident in the actual and figurative transformation of the dead at wakes and burial sites and the changing periphery of death on the urban and suburban landscape through home shrines, cemetery locations, roadside memorials, museum exhibitions, and Day of the Dead festivities.

The present dialogue on the nexus between ancients and moderns began as a personal quest for the meaning and relevance of traditional rites in a modern multicultural world. The focus is on death, disposal, and commemoration, rather than dying, across temporal, geographic and cultural lines. The dialogue depends on a long line of the dead, their mourners, and their commemorators from antiquity to the present. A short interdisciplinary study as the current volume can only include a few of them as representatives of diverse groups practising diverse rites. As the diversity of rites grows and awareness of others' rites heightens, more voices will join the conversation and contribute to the legacy.

CHAPTER I

FUNERALS

If my family has an open casket, I want to be fixed up to the max.
I want to look good. I want them to fill in my wrinkles; I want people
to say, 'God, she looks great. She looks better dead than alive.'[1]

Reversing the physical transformations of death, whether natural or traumatic, is associated with open coffin viewings in order to make the deceased recognizable or look 'at peace'. To offset decomposition, lips, cheeks, and hands are often filled for public viewing but the wish to be made more attractive or youthful in death, however, is paradoxical.[2] Rather than reconstructive surgery, this post-mortem elective surgery seems self-indulgent: the comfort and peace of mind of mourners in viewing the deceased restored to their former appearance of just days prior to death is exchanged for a dramatic revelation of a body transformed to their ideal or to the appearance of their youth.[3] The theatricality inherent in the display and viewing of the dead leads to the ethical questions of how should one look in death and whether one should even look upon the dead?

Ancient Greek and Roman funerary practices have shaped Western attitudes towards death and the dead. Although, like the ancients, we distance ourselves from death, we continue to engage in ongoing social relationships with the dead. This paradox is grounded in the biology of death and the sociology of human relationships with the dead: corpses decay and need to be disposed of but we continue to attach the former personality and

1

identity to the body. This chapter explores how modern funerary practices, from preparing a corpse for visitation to the events leading up to disposal, share ancient strategies for avoiding contact with death while preserving the identity of the dead for continued relationships with the living. Modern paradigms are shifting due to cultural preferences and the increasing role of the internet in making various aspects of funerals available to a wider audience.

Funeral paradigms

Funerals are important events in demarcating but also in erasing boundaries between the living and the dead. As a formulaic event experienced by many, it is nonetheless difficult to summarize typical elements due to individual preferences and varying cultural and religious rites that are themselves evolving into new paradigms. The term funeral is broad and refers to the series of events that leads to disposal: a wake, with or without an open coffin, a memorial or religious service, and disposal, whether cremation or an inhumation burial. Conveyance of the deceased to the burial site in a vehicle or carried by mourners may also be part of the burial ritual. Depending on one's culture, religion, or individual preferences, however, not all of these elements may be present. Jewish funerary customs, for example, do not allow embalming and call for burial as soon as possible after death. Funerals are formulaic, therefore, but variations to the paradigm evolve without obscuring the primary function of the ritual.

In a public funeral, preparations and display events are centred on both the deceased and mourners. The embalming or washing of the corpse, for example, is not necessary for disposal but it preserves the deceased for a public viewing that allows mourners an opportunity to socialize with the body of the deceased for a final time. Visitation also allows mourners to process the death psychologically and emotionally as they accept or express condolences. This reciprocity reinforces the life cycle with its perennial demands on the living to bury the dead and to reintegrate with society after a period of mourning. The wake emerges as a liminal experience for both the deceased and survivors, in particular for maintaining social relationships with the dead.

Religion may or may not be a factor in modern funerals: laws and ordinances prescribe the sanitary conditions by which funerals are carried out but they do not dictate religious observance. That does not mean, however, that one's religious customs cannot be affected by legislation. Immigrants may need to combine traditional rites with those of their new country and indigenous culture, especially if traditional rites, such as outdoor cremations, clash with local or state ordinances that dictate that they be held indoors at an approved facility.[4] Alternately, an atheist may choose to have a secular service but a member of a religious community may opt for sacred rites and a religious service.

Burial and mourning were subject to legislation in ancient Athens and Rome.[5] Implicit and explicit reasons seem to be for the observance of religious rites, community hygiene, and to curb excessive displays of grief or expenditure that could promote political ambition and social unrest. In other words, laws governed the disposal of the deceased but also the behaviour and appearance of mourners, especially if paid, which could be an indicator of wealth and social status. In his *Life of Solon* (21.4–5), Plutarch describes Solon's reforms that are mostly aimed at curbing the activities of women in public at both funerals and festivals. Prohibitions at funerals included wearing no more than three articles of clothing, the carrying of no more than one obol's worth of food or drink, a pannier of no more than a cubit in height and no travel at night except by wagon with their way lit by a lamp. Lacerations of the flesh by mourners were forbidden, as were ritual lamentations (*threnos*), and the bewailing of anyone at the funeral ceremonies of another.[6] How does one observe or enforce a law that curbs human emotion? Was incredible self-control maintained in observance of law or were spontaneous (and potentially violent) expressions of grief overlooked if not considered intentionally attention-seeking? In the late fourth century BCE, Demetrios of Phaleron made changes to Solon's laws to curb the growing excess in funerals and burials since their passage. Demetrios' reforms suggest that the earlier attempt to legislate grief was difficult to enforce, but it is impossible to know how closely his own were observed.[7]

Roman funerary and burial laws outlined in the Twelve Tables curbed excessive expressions of grief by forbidding such activities as digging up a corpse for the staging of multiple funerals. Excessive expressions of power or wealth were curbed through the limiting of expenses to three veils, a purple tunic, and ten flute players. The funerals of aristocrats (discussed below) were orchestrated events with mimes, the display of ancestor portraits, and scenic entertainment, so it seems that there were still opportunities for families to engage in the promotion of the individual or clan (*gens*). Other laws prohibited cremation or burial within the (sacred) boundary of the city (*pomerium*), but exceptions are known such as the graves of city heroes, whether legendary or historical, or children (Chapter III).[8] Cicero's *De legibus* is the main source for the citation of these laws, such as the law that a grave only obtained legal and religious status after the sacrifice of a pig at the site of burial.[9] Unfortunately, most of the laws that Cicero cites outline what cannot be done, rather than describe the funerary and burial customs that were actually practised by contemporaries.

Today in the West, social customs and/or religion, rather than legislation usually govern the appropriate clothing to wear at a funeral or during the period of mourning. The wearing of black or dark colours at a funeral is customary in Western cultures but in the East, white is associated with mourning. Wearing mourning clothing for an extended period depends on one's culture and religion. Immigration further complicates the reading of colour within and across cultures. The symbolism attached to the colour black is changing since its popularity in fashion makes it difficult to know if someone is in mourning. Black clothing is likely to signal a woman in mourning in the Mediterranean region but a fashionable woman at a cocktail party in Manhattan. This marks a distinct change from the elaborate and codified mourning clothing in the Victorian era in which the demand for black crape and other clothing items supported a mourning industry.[10]

Funeral homes do not post the same dress codes as retail stores do, such as the display of a sign on the door with an 'X' over bare feet, but the social

4

expectation is for attendees to wear clothing, however casual, to be respectful of the occasion. Dress codes may be more formal at religious services as clergy may expect worshippers and funeral attendees to cover their knees and shoulders and perhaps even for women to wear a veil. Dress codes, however, are still imposed in some countries to limit the expression of political dissidence at public funerals. In Iran, for example, supporters of the Green Revolution in 2009 were forbidden to wear or carry green symbols in support of the Revolution at the funeral of Grand Ayatollah Hossein Ali Montazeri. Many mourners, however, disobeyed the prohibition and with green symbols, chanted anti-government slogans, risking arrest, injury, and even death.

Death on the periphery

Death is a biological and a social construct that makes the moment of death, the transformation from body to corpse, difficult to define.[11] Does death occur when the heart or brain ceases to function? Or does death occur at a later point such as after the performance of ritual, as among Hindus who define death as the moment when the skull (during cremation) is cracked and releases the soul?[12] Interaction and continuing relationships with the dead in Western societies depend on viewing a corpse as the embodiment of pollution (the antithesis of a healthy living body) but also as the focus of materiality that allows for the socializing of the body by the living. Open coffin funerals play an important role in maintaining social relationships with the dead. Definitions of self, body, and soul affect the living's interaction with the dead: embalming humanizes the dead body and effects a transformation from defiling corpse to a body representing the former living body and person.[13] The powerless corpse also attains a symbolic power that is subject to exploitation to advance various agendas of the living.[14]

Viewing the corpse as a source of environmental or religious pollution has deep cultural roots. In ancient Greece and Rome, religion played an important role in funerals and the burial of the dead was a sacred rite that had consequences for the deceased in the afterlife if a body was either not buried, whether on land or at sea, or not buried properly.[15] Pollution could also attach to the sacred places of the gods if contaminated by corpses that were brought into the city.[16]

Infamous cases of corpse abuse in ancient Rome were usually politically motivated from denial of burial, decapitation in the cases of Pompey the Great, Brutus, Cicero, and the emperor Galba to corpse abuse (Sejanus' corpse was dragged by a hook to the Tiber) and the desecration of funeral and burial rites: the charred body of Pompey's father was pulled from his bier during cremation and Sulla had Marius' remains dug up and thrown into the Anio river.[17] Abuse could also extend to the deceased's memory with the destruction of their images and any epigraphic traces.[18]

Exposure to corpses also had consequences for the living. While it was important to prepare someone for burial, it was also important for the public to avoid the sight of or contact with corpses. Houses in mourning in early Greece were indicated by sprays of celery, laurel, marjoram, and myrtle.[19] For the Classical period in Athens, a jar was placed outside the door with water from an outside source. The jar served to warn strangers of a death in the house but the water was also used by family members to purify themselves on leaving.[20] Later, a lock of hair or cypress on the door indicated a death in the family. In the *Alcestis* (438 BCE), Euripides dramatizes a breach in funerary custom involving a death in the house: Herakles arrives at the palace of Admetus following Alcestis' death yet is nonetheless entertained by Ademetus who does not inform him that the house is in mourning. At issue is Admetus' role as host and Herakles' un-intentional offensive drunken behaviour. When sacrifices are performed at Alcestis' tomb, Herakles makes amends by ambushing Death and securing Alcestis' return to life.

In ancient Rome, houses in mourning (*funesta*) were marked with branches of cypress and pine for nine days.[21] Of particular concern was the health of the urban environment but religious motivations can also be detected: just as in ancient Athens where *demarchoi* removed abandoned corpses and purified the demes that had been polluted, at Rome, *aediles* were responsible for removing corpses from city streets in the late first century BCE. Roman magistrates and priests were distanced from death pollution. Funeral professionals, such as undertakers (*libitinarii*), ushers (*dissignatores*), morticians (*pollinctores*), bier carriers of the less wealthy (*vespilliones*), cremators (*ustores*), grave diggers (*fossores*), and flute players, who performed at funerals, served as mediators between the living and the polluting dead. Their services were located in the Grove of Libitina outside the Esquiline Gate (Porta Esquilina), and subject to special legislation.[22] A section of a law from the town of Puteoli that may be similar to Roman law demarcates where funeral professionals may live and the manner in which they may enter the city:

> The workers who are to provide this service are not to live on this side of the tower where the grove of Libitina is today and are to bathe after the first hour of the night. They are not to enter the town except for the purpose of carrying off and relocating corpses, or exacting punishment. While and as often as in this way one of them comes to, enters, or is in the town he should have on his head a red cap.[23]

The red cap serves as a warning sign to the public not to come into contact with funeral professionals.

Funeral professionals are not shunned today in Western societies but modern rural Cantonese funeral workers (*pai shih*) are subjected to similar residential isolation and strict working regulations as their ancient counterparts to prevent death pollution.[24] Undertakers, for example, are ranked according to the extent of their contact with the dead, with greater contact resulting in more pollution, and are only permitted to enter the community to conduct funerals. A shared culture of ancestor worship between ancient Romans and Cantonese may explain similarities in their practices that do not endure in the West.

Staging the dead

Theatre metaphors connect the preparation of the corpse and the visitation to theatrical events complete with actor, audience, and stage. In many cultures, funeral professionals are responsible for the viewing and disposal of the dead that begins with turning a cadaver back into a body. Survivors may provide a photograph, clothing, and hairstyle information but it the mortician who effects the transformation:

> It is the embalmer's role to re-establish the body's boundaries. In arresting decomposition and shoring up its physical boundaries, the worker restores the body's social and conceptual boundaries. On the practical level this entails removing the most obvious signs of death that linger, and can be observed on the body. After death the body loses the human qualities associated with vitality: it lacks vigour, the skin becomes discoloured and slack, the hair limp, limbs are stiff and inactive and further deterioration is inevitable as decomposition rapidly erodes the organs and tissues. If the deceased is to regain any semblance of individuality, the decay must be halted, the body preserved, albeit temporarily, and its human features redeemed.[25]

Several days may pass before the deceased is ready for viewing to allow time for embalming, reconstructive surgery, or forensic procedures such as an autopsy.[26] During this time, the deceased is isolated from family members until the time of viewing. Proper preparation is essential since modern wakes may last for several days with multiple visitations that can last from one to several hours.

The period of embalming is also a time when families must trust professionals for the proper and respectful care of loved ones.[27] Abuse of this trust does happen, however, and makes for shocking news headlines. A recent criminal probe, for example, confirmed rumours circulating for years that the body of James Hines was cut to fit his coffin. Family members thought that the coffin was too small for Hines who was a 6'7", 300-pound preacher and funk musician from Allendale, South Carolina. Hines' widow said that investigators who exhumed his body, which was buried in 2004, told her that 'his legs had been cut off between the ankle and calf, and his feet had been placed inside the casket.'[28] In another instance, relatives who arrived at a funeral home in Stickney, Illinois for the visitation of their 91-year-old grandmother Lillian Grogan discovered the wrong body in the coffin wearing her dress and favourite bracelet.[29] Grogan's body, which had been mistakenly buried before the visitation, was exhumed and reburied.

In ancient Egypt, embalming was performed by professional embalmers as part of the process of mummification to preserve the body for burial and the afterlife, rather than for visitation.[30] The Greek historian Herodotus (2.85) precedes his description of embalming with a brief account of mourning and funerary rituals to emphasize even more differences between the two cultures: prior to embalming, the women in the household of a distinguished man smeared their heads or faces with mud. Then they left the body inside as they roamed the streets with the dead man's female relatives. They fastened their dresses with a girdle but they beat their bared breasts. Men also wore a girdle and beat their breasts. After this mourning ritual, they returned home to take the body to be embalmed.

Herodotus (2. 86–89) describes various embalming methods that varied depending on procedure and price: the most perfect method involves removal of the brain through the nostrils with an iron hook and rinsing the rest with drugs. An incision was made in the abdomen and the contents removed. The cavity was then cleansed and washed with palm wine and spices and then filled with grounded spices: myrrh, cassia, and other spices except frankincense. The body was next sewn up and covered in natrum for seventy days and afterwards washed and wrapped from head to toe with strips of linen coated on the underside with gum. The body was then returned to the family who placed it in a wooden case, shaped like a human figure, which was sealed and positioned upright in a burial chamber.

A second option was less expensive and involved no incision and removal of the intestines but only the injection of cedar oil into the body through the anus that was then stopped up to prevent the fluid from escaping. After the body was placed in natrum for the required number of days, they released the oil whose effect was so powerful that it carries away with it the stomach and intestines in a liquid state. The natrum also dissolved the flesh leaving only bones and skin in which state the embalmers returned the body without doing anything further. The third option was the least expensive for the poor and involved cleaning out the intestines with a purge, placing the body in natrum for seventy days and then returning the body to be taken away without doing anything further. In an interesting parallel to the level of trust required of modern embalmers by grieving family members, Herodotus records that the bodies of distinguished or beautiful women were given to embalmers after three or four days had passed to ensure that the body would not be violated by them. The practice was occasioned by an incident of necrophilia that was reported by the embalmer's colleague.

In ancient Rome, the infamous embalming of Nero's second wife Poppaea Sabina suggests that it offended traditional mores.[31] Earlier, Mark Antony's body was presumably embalmed and buried alongside Cleopatra, but that was in Egypt, not Rome. During the Roman period of Egyptian history, Romans received burials in the local manner with portraits painted on wooden panels that were wrapped in the cartonnage in a remarkable synthesis of native Roman and native Egyptian funerary rites.[32]

Internal embalming should be distinguished from the external application of substances onto the body to preserve the flesh for a sarcophagus burial.[33] It is not known how prevalent the practice of applying a preservative coat was in ancient Rome when inhumation burials became more prevalent, but the cost of both a sarcophagus and the preservatives may have limited such a burial to the wealthy.

In April 1485, the body of a young woman, once identified as Cicero's daughter Tulliola, was discovered along the Via Appia in a remarkable state of preservation due to a thick application of preservatives composed of myrrh, balm, and cedar oil. The preservatives were highly effective in arresting the decomposition of the flesh for several days until its removal. Given the large amounts used and their potential attraction to bees (as happened when the body was displayed), it is unlikely that she was displayed at her funeral with such a thick application of substances. This does not preclude, however, that ointments and other fragrances were added to the body previously to preserve the body and minimize odour for visitation. After her sarcophagus was opened, she was put on display on the Capitoline Hill (Chapter IV).[34]

In the US, embalming in the manner of a mummy is attracting interest as a burial option. References to ancient Egypt include an embalming facility in the shape of a pyramid.[35] Framing a modern death in relation to ancient Egyptian practices is intentional but it is out of its original religious context. Even the mortuary setting is altered: rather than serve as a resting place, the pyramid serves as the preparation facility prior to burial elsewhere.

Modern funeral homes in the West as locations for staged and performed events extend the theatricality inherent in preserving a body for visitation. The transformation of the deceased through embalming, for example, is followed by display in a staged setting amidst visitation activities that place the focus on the deceased in the coffin.[36] The 'home-like' setting evokes a formal living room or parlour but the setting is clearly not home and is recognizable as the setting for wakes. Not only is the deceased lying in state in a recreated living room rather than a bedroom, but the backdrop of flowers and floral tributes in vases, pots, and stands evokes a hospital room or even a religious shrine.[37] The line between visitation and theatre, however, was explicitly crossed at the wake of actor Leslie Nielsen. Guests received invitations to his memorial that was billed as 'Cocktails with Leslie and Barbaree' at the Lago Mar Resort, Fort Lauderdale, FL.[38] As jazz music played, guests milled around the open coffin with drinks in hand as clips from his comedy films played on a giant screen. The dramatic illusion of the event as a cocktail party hosted by the deceased and his wife was shattered when some of the guests wept openly. The 'entertaining corpse' at their own funeral is part of an ancient tradition in which the deceased served as host at their grave (Chapter IV).

The positioning of the deceased is part of the staging of wakes and coffin presentation. In modern Western coffin burials or open coffin wakes, the deceased is commonly lying in state in a supine posture with face upwards.

The posture, however, is not universal and exceptions are noteworthy. When the vault above Marilyn Monroe at the Westwood Village Memorial Park was auctioned on eBay, the widow whose husband had occupied the vault placed the following advertisement: 'Here is a once in a lifetime and into eternity opportunity to spend your eternal days directly above Marilyn Monroe. In fact, the person occupying the address right now is looking face down on her.'[39]

Sandra Ilene West, Beverly Hills socialite and Texas oil heiress, set the standard for non-traditional body positions and burials in the US when she was buried at the Alamo Masonic Cemetery in San Antonio, Texas on 10 March 1977. She was seated behind the wheel of her powder-blue Ferrari 330 America with the seat reclined at a 'comfortable angle' as specified in her will and dressed in a black negligee. West and the car are buried in a container that measures 6×8×17 feet and which was filled with concrete to prevent vandalism.

Other recent examples of non-traditional body positions are equally remarkable for presenting the deceased as still alive in a social setting. The position and surroundings are part of a larger agenda of celebrating life in addition to marking death. The body of 24-year-old Angel Pantoja Medina was embalmed in a standing position and dressed in his everyday clothes including a baseball cap and sunglasses for his three-day wake at the home of his mother in San Juan, Puerto Rico.[40] The deceased's mother claimed to be fulfilling her son's wish and the result was a social gathering rather than a sombre wake, at which mourners could socialize with the deceased one final time. When the deceased is among the mourners as one of them rather than the focus of a lying-in-state display, especially standing in the corner of a living room, the line between the living and the dead becomes blurred. The same funeral home that prepared the body of Angel Pantoja Medina, the Marin Funeral Home in San Juan, Puerto Rico, recently embalmed the body of 22-year-old David Morales Colón seated on his Honda CBR600 F4 motorcycle.[41] The deceased is riding his motorcycle seemingly to reach heaven at full speed wearing a baseball cap and sunglasses with his helmet on the seat next to him and positioned between two candelabra.

Modern theme displays in funeral homes make the theatre setting of visitations more explicit as they make generic funeral home parlours suited to an individual's personality and actual home setting. The atmosphere is far from sombre but rather 'lively' as a celebration of the deceased's life and personality. Theme funerals share similarities with 'theme weddings' especially in the case of the bride metaphor that makes connections between two rites explicit. The 'Big Mama' visitation theme at the Wade Funeral Home, St. Louis, MO allows the deceased to (re)assume role playing. The coffin sits in the middle of a stage setting with a kitchen table, refrigerator and stove with food such as gumbo and pie ready to eat. Mourners are invited to treat the funeral parlour as the kitchen of the deceased, who continues to entertain guests and includes the repast or funeral meal within the visitation (Chapter IV). The display is set up within the space normally decorated as a formal parlour but the backdrop does not block out windows behind the false partition wall and the setting looks like a merchandise display in the front window of a retail store. Themes such as the 'Sportsman' with fishing, hunting and camping gear arranged around the coffin also evoke retail display settings. Amidst these props, the deceased assumes the role of an actor before a (re)acting audience of mourners who participate in the staged recreation of the deceased's former and current life.

Viewing the dead

In the Staglieno Cemetery (Cimitero monumentale di Staglieno or Camposanto di Staglieno), Genoa, the funerary monument of Raffaele Pienovi (1879) by Giovanni Battista Villa depicts his second wife Virginia gently lifting a corner of the sheet that covers her husband's face [**Fig. 1**]. The scene is a tender one as the widow uncovers the face for one final look before burial. The wife, impeccably dressed in period clothing, dutifully attends to her husband's body with a loving expression that does not show signs of excessive grief. The focus is on the mourner rather than the deceased whose face is barely visible to signify her perpetual mourning at the site of burial (as representative and symbol of family grief).[42] The monument

Fig. 1. Funerary Monument of Raffaele Pienovi. Staglieno Cemetery, Genoa.

is at once an example of bourgeois realism but it is also emblematic of the rites performed by wives in their own parlours and by their sculptural representations that play out the same scene at the tombs of their husbands in Staglieno and other cemeteries such as Campo Verano Cemetery, Rome. The effect is one of contemporaneous wakes, ostensibly set in parlours, amidst other Victorian burial monuments that line porticoes. The mourners appear as period actors on a raised podium vying for the attention of modern-day cemetery visitors who seem to stroll through successive theatre sets.

In ancient Greece, the preparation of the corpse for viewing and burial was done in the home and was the responsibility of women.[43] No single literary source describes elements of a typical Greek funeral so variations in the following summary should be assumed depending on the status of the deceased, the historical period, and location of their death. At the house of the deceased, women washed the corpse and anointed it with oil. Without modern embalming techniques to preserve the corpse, this centuries-old process must have been sufficient to preserve the body for visitation until the burial.

The washing of the corpse in Islamic funerals is an essential ritual of the Sunnah of the Prophet Muhammad and part of the Islamic Sharia. The lack of exposure of the deceased and direct contact with the body varies from ancient Greek practices. As soon as possible after death, the body is draped with a cloth and then washed by family members of the same sex. The cloth remains on the body during washing as water is poured through the cloth. The genitals remain covered the whole time. The body is wrapped in a plain cotton or linen cloth shroud (*kafan*) that is usually white but the colour may vary. Perfume may be added to the cloth to preserve the body for visitation and prayers (*Salat al-Janazah*) that may last a few hours before the deceased is conveyed for burial as soon as possible after death. Under extraordinary circumstances exceptions are possible. The naked body of deposed dictator Muammar Ghadafi was displayed in a meat freezer for sevaral days to give Libyans an opportunity to verify his death.

With the rise of at-home funerals (as opposed to funeral home events), in North America, there is also an increase in washing and displaying the body at home without embalming. This form of direct involvement in the caring of the dead reflects a choice that resembles traditional and modern burial customs in the Mediterranean and Middle East but one that may not be religious in nature. Home funerals are also a return to the traditional practice of home funerals in Europe and North America that were moved to funeral homes and subsequently regulated following the outbreak of cholera and other diseases.[44] Foregoing embalming and visitation – which are not legally required in many states (as opposed to the procurement of a death certificate and permission to transport the body for disposition) – has meant relearning rituals and skills long handed over to professionals.[45] Ironically, home funerals transform the home into a funeral home that is itself an evocation of the home.

After the washing of the corpse in ancient Greece, the eyes were closed to evoke sleeping and perhaps even for the living to avert the potentially dangerous gaze of the dead. A coin was placed between the teeth to ensure payment to the ferryman Charon for the journey to the Underworld. For the wealthy, after a chinstrap made of cloth or gold was attached and a crown placed on the head, the body was dressed. Clothing was usually white and may have changed in time from an ankle-length robe to a shroud (*endyma*) or loose covering (*epiblêma*). Legislation, such as the law code of Ioulis on Keos, dictated the amount of money that could be spent on the clothing to prevent ostentation. The bodies of the unmarried or recently married were dressed in wedding clothes and soldiers of the Geometric period were buried with armour or a military cloak (*phoinikis*) in the case of Spartans.

What follows the washing and the dressing of the corpse is remarkably similar to modern funeral home visitations and the dramatic illusions of presenting a corpse before a mourning audience. Some particulars may be different but in general, the acts of mourning and disposal are perennially played out like a drama on a changing stage with actors that keep close to the primordial script. The body, as though the deceased were asleep, was then placed on a bier made to look like a bed. The deceased was positioned

Fig. 2. Terracotta Krater. Attr. Hirschfield Workshop. Inv. 14.130.14.
The Metropolitan Museum of Art, New York.

with feet facing the door in preparation for lying in state (*prothesis*) and ritual mourning by female family members or professionals that included personal (*góos*) and formal ritual lamentation (*threnos*) accompanied by raising of hands, the tearing of hair, the scratching of cheeks, and the beating of breasts.[46] At the foot of the bier, men performed the valediction. A terracotta krater (c. 750–735 BCE) attributed to the Hirschfield Workshop in the Metropolitan Museum of Art, New York (Inv. 14.130.14) that served as a tomb marker depicts a scene of *prothesis* [**Fig. 2**]. The stylized scene presents the deceased lying on a couch and surrounded on each side by women mourners who tear at their hair. Other figures are seated or stand next to the deceased and a procession of chariots and footsoldiers occupy a lower band. The simplicity of the depictions does not detract from its emotive force. Graveside offerings could be poured into the krater on the day of burial and on subsequent days following burial and on annual festivals (Chapter IV).

Before dawn, the deceased was conveyed from the home to the place of burial in a quiet procession (*ekphora*) that may have later included hired musicians. Professionals could be hired to help the family carry the corpse (*klimakophoroi*; *nekrophoroi*) and to perform the burial (*nekrothaptai*; *tapheis*). The procession brought funeral rituals outdoors and was subject to legislation to ensure the orderly disposal of the dead when there were few people on the streets to witness the corpse or mourners.[47] Men walked before the women to the grave at which laws forbade ceremonies and large sacrifices, such as oxen, following burial; but the offering of smaller animals, fruits, grain, flowers, and libations was practised (Chapter II). According to Plutarch (*Solon* 21.5), family members were forbidden to visit the tombs of others at the time of interment, which may explain the popularity of *prothesis* and other funeral scenes on pottery and plaques at the site of burial (Chapter IV).

The historical sources for ancient Roman funerals are incomplete and one cannot assume universality of practice in a society centred on social status with a diversity of religious beliefs. The attitudes and practices of the wealthy often eclipse those of the poor. Moreover, diachronic accuracy is difficult due to the vast gaps in the evidence from different time periods under the Republic and Empire. The following may be representative: obsequies began on the deathbed: the household head (*pater familias*) or heir, if present, would place the body of the dying person on the ground and catch the last breath with a kiss.[48] The eyes of the deceased were closed and those present would shout their name (*conclamatio*). As with Greek funeral preparations, women probably washed and anointed the corpse on the floor and prepared it for visitation. Depending on the financial means of a family, funeral professionals could aid the women in preparing the corpse for viewing but they were most likely used in assisting burial. If the deceased was a male citizen, he was dressed in a white tunic and toga. Women were dressed in long tunics or in wedding attire adorned with jewellery and a wreath. The body was placed on a couch, as though asleep, with feet facing the door.

Surrounding the deceased were funeral lights, torches and/or candelabra that were kept burning until burial. For the wealthy, the lying-in-state ceremony (*collocatio*) was held in the atrium of the house, with ritual lamentation at intervals until disposal, which could be as long as seven days after death. Reliefs from the Tomb of the Haterii (late first century CE/early second century CE) depict various stages of the funeral of a woman on her bier surrounded by mourners, musicians, and torches.[49] The poor were cremated or buried more quickly and with less ceremony. It is likely that they were carried off for cremation or burial soon after death. Differences in burial practices among pagans and Christians do not seem to extend to the preparation of the corpse for visitation, whose elements share long-standing similarities with Greek rituals.

Traditional Sikh funerary rituals (*antam sanskar*) that share many features with Hindu rites in Punjab are remarkably similar to ancient Greek and Roman practices.[50] Last rite rituals begin with dying on the ground (*dharti tey pauna*) since dying in bed is a symbol of neglect and a source of social shame that requires an act of purification (*gati*) to release the soul. A lamp is lit near the deceased if the death occurs during the night. The deceased's family and members of one's caste (*biradari*) remain in the room and the doors of the house are opened to allow the release of the soul. They next prepare the body for cremation with a ritual bath (*antam ishnan*) that purifies the deceased from the pollution of death. After dressing the deceased in new clothes, the body is placed on a bier. If a wife dies before her husband, she is dressed as a bride. Last respects are paid to the deceased by touching the feet and sometimes placing money on the bier.

Sons or brothers of the deceased usually carry the bier to cremation led by the eldest son (or in his absence, a younger brother or paternal uncle) who functions as chief mourner. Although women form part of the funeral procession, they do not participate in this carrying ritual (*modha dena*) since it is connected with ancient rules of inheritance. Near the site of cremation, the body is lowered to the ground and starting from the head, the chief mourner pours water from an earthen pot in an unbroken circle around the deceased (*dhamalak bhanana*). The pot is then smashed onto the ground to symbolize the release of the soul. From this point, women are forbidden from entering the cremation ground.

The bier is carried to the cremation ground and placed on a pyre that is lit by the deceased's son. In India, male members of the household and caste collect the ashes on the third day following the funeral and take them to Hardwar to be deposited in the river Ganges with the assistance of a Brahmin. Thirteen days after the funeral, the son participates in a ritual feast (*akath*) with relatives and caste members to receive a new turban (*pagri*) and assume his new position as head of the household.

Likening the dead

Literary descriptions of funerals and ritual mourning appear as early as Homer's *Iliad* (Patroklos and Hector) and *Odyssey* (Penelope's suitors) and the epic poem the *Little Iliad* (Ajax). These narratives of death rites served as the source of allusion and intertextuality for later Greek and Latin literature, such as tragedy and epic poetry, and art from Greek vase painting and steles to Roman sarcophagi. Latin literary descriptions of death ritual, such as the preparation of the corpse, construction of a pyre and reenactments of ritual mourning are also literary allusions to ritual practice, therefore caution should be taken into reading these funerals as evidence or prescriptions for actual funerals.[51]

An early example of women's expression of grief in the *Iliad* may also reveal the prohibition to its expression in public more suited to the funerary culture in Athens at the time that the poem was given written form. When Priam returns to Troy with Hector's body, he delays the women from mourning him at the city gates and urges them to offer lamentation in the palace. After the lamentation (*threnos*) of the professional mourners that Homer does not cite, comes the lament (*góos*) of Andromache that contains both praise and reproach for her husband.[52] Andromache is then followed by Hecuba and Helen. These laments for Hector are at once literary examples (rather than verbatim quotations) and symbols of lamentation that form a long tradition of oral poetry and performance to contemporary Greek lamentations.[53]

The framing of contemporary tastes in relation to Homer and subsequent Greek and Latin variations seems to have provided a means by which to universalize shared or personal experiences and emotions to a wider audience. In this way, Aeschylus' Electra offering a libation at the grave of her father Agamemnon in the *Libation Bearers* serves the same allusive function as figures on Attic vases visiting graves to actual mourners performing graveside rituals. (Self-) identification is expressed through the shared metaphor by which the allusions serve to mythologize or to elevate contemporary referents (one receives a funeral appropriate of a Patroklos or a Hector) and emotions (one has suffered or mourns a loss like a Hecuba). Since these analogies are suggestive rather than determinative, their interpretation allows for varying and subjective identifications (and deviations) of similar qualities and experiences.[54] The funeral of another, whether figurative or real, may encourage rather than limit personal or personalizing expression.[55] This may be especially true in the case of women whose public mourning practices became more restricted following the Archaic period.

In addition to likening the deceased to the mythological and literary dead, one may also liken burial rites themselves to other rites, such as marriage rites. Modern Greek lamentations extend the analogy that connects death rites to marriage rites. In a lament from Potamia, the dying man uses an extended metaphor of a wedding to the earth to announce his death to his wife and family:

> You young shepherds, you unfortunate young men,
> tomorrow you will go back to our village, to our desolate homeland.
> Don't fire your rifles. Don't sing any songs.
> Don't let my brothers and sisters hear you.
> Don't let my wife or my poor grandchildren hear you.
> Don't tell them that I have been killed.
> > Don't tell them that I am dead.
> Just tell them that I have married and taken a good wife.
> I have taken the tombstone as my mother-in-law, the black earth as
> > my wife,
> and I have the little pebbles as brothers- and sisters-in-law.[56]

Likening the dead to brides and burial to a wedding further extends the metaphors associated with ritual transformations – from figurative initiations and rites of passage to literal departures away from the home to a new one.[57] The burial of unmarried or engaged girls in bridal attire evokes a wedding never celebrated but the burial and commemoration of married women as brides evokes and repeats an actual event. The depiction of matrons as brides clasping the right hand of her husband on Roman funerary reliefs advertises her status through referencing the rite that first changed both her status and home.

In ancient and modern Greece, funeral rites may be framed as a wedding through explicit and implicit signifiers: women (young and old) laid out as a bride for the *prothesis*, mourned by funeral lamentations that bear similarities to songs that mark the departure of the bride. In one lamentation, a dying girl compares Death (Charos/Charon) to a bridegroom coming to take her away from her family. Her mother, however, rebukes her and hands her over to him.[58] The dead girl, like the bride, leaves the home of her father and grieving mother bearing money or gifts. Lamentations sung at the grave (*moirologia*) also evoke wedding songs with shared poetic meters and themes of departure and death.[59]

Evidence for burying women as brides extends to ancient Rome. During the construction of the Palazzo di Giustizia in Rome, a sarcophagus was found containing the skeletal remains of a young woman, Crepereia Tryphaena, who died at the beginning of the third century CE.[60] The young woman was dressed as a bride with a bridal crown of myrtle leaves that were well preserved. She wore a ring engraved with the name of her betrothed Philetus. Placed next to her were a chest with cosmetics and a wooden doll that brides offered as gifts to Venus or Diana on their wedding day. Remarkably, Crepereia Tryphaena's head drooped to the left just as the head of the female figure displayed for visitation in the relief on the sarcophagus.

Not all associations between weddings and funerals are figurative. In a chilling evocation of the myth of Polyxena who was sacrificed at the tomb of Achilles to be his bride in death, police in China uncovered a crime ring that murdered women to serve as brides for dead bachelors.[61] The first victim was a mentally handicapped woman whose family thought they were paying for her to be married to a live husband. The purchaser murdered the woman after selling her through an intermediary to the father of a dead son. Apparently, the unfortunate woman was worth more dead than alive. The ring corrupted the Chinese custom now only practised in poor rural areas of burying a recently dead young woman next to a dead son as his wife (*minghun*) after paying her family a 'dowry'. The status of the couple and their families change and they consider themselves in-laws. These 'ghost marriages' mirror the practice of buying a bride for a son and are still prevalent in poor remote areas of Shanxi and Shaanxi provinces.

Animating the dead

An important distinction between Greek and Roman aristocratic funerals was the making of wax portraits called *imagines* prior to disposal.[62] These life-like portraits were carried in procession or worn as a mask by mime actors at the funeral and later displayed in the atrium of the house in shrines among the *imagines* of ancestors until the next family funeral. The renaissance death mask of Lorenzo de Medici may give some indication of their appearance.[63] From the wax portrait or the mould that made them, a marble or bronze portrait bust or statue could be made, sometimes many years after death to advertise family connections.[64] The display of these portraits illustrates, literally and figuratively, that funerals in Rome were performed events versus funerals in Athens whose laws forbade public ceremony.

While embalming preserves the body/identity of the deceased for a few days to allow for visitation inside a funeral home, the making of a wax mask preserves the face/identity of the deceased for ancestor worship, religious ceremonies, and future participation in the funerals of descendants; that is, display in public areas within and outside the home in repeated appearances. Both of these ancient and modern ceremonies centre on the animation of the corpse within a theatricalized setting: an acting corpse before mourners who also perform the simultaneous roles of actor audience. The symbolic reintegration of the dead in the home following a funeral and as participants in the funerals of their descendants points to the on-going social relationships between the living and the dead evident even in modern Day of the Dead celebrations (Chapter IV).

Roman aristocrats participated in an elaborate funeral procession (*pompa*) that could include the carrying or wearing of ancestor portraits, musicians, and professional mourners.[65] Etruscan, rather than Greek practice, which forbade public processions, influenced these processions. Funeral games (scenic/gladiatorial) and eulogies (*laudatio*) in the Roman Forum could form part of the funeral and provide the elite with an opportunity for the promotion of their clan (*gens*).[66] At the grave, a libation was poured and a sacrificial meal prepared for the dead and shared by the mourners. The sacrifice of a pig was also necessary. Subsequent graveside rituals took place on the ninth day after the funeral and on anniversary and annual festivals devoted to the dead, such as the *Parentalia* and *Feralia*, on which food offerings were made and shared with the dead (Chapter IV).

In a famous passage describing an elite funeral from the Republican period, the historian Polybius gives a generalising picture of a theatricalized ceremony that integrates the living with the dead:

> Whenever any famous man dies, he is carried in a funeral procession to the so-called rostra in the forum sometimes in an upright position, rarely prostrate. With all of the populace standing around, a son, if he is alive and happens to be present, or if not, some other relative, steps up onto the rostra and speaks about the virtues and accomplishments achieved in the lifetime of the deceased. [. . .] Next comes the burial and the performance of the customary ceremonies and they place an image of the deceased in the most conspicuous part of the house, setting it in a wooden shrine. This image is a mask, a completely accurate recreation of his face, similar in appearance and features. They lovingly decorate these images and display them for public sacrifices and whenever a famous member of the family dies, they carry them to the funeral, placing them on those whom they consider to most resemble the deceased in size and posture. These men wear togas bordered by purple if the deceased was a consul or praetor, a purple toga if a censor, and embroidered with gold if he had celebrated a triumph or had achieved anything similar. They ride on chariots and carried before them are fasces, axes, and the customary things that accompany magistrates according to the dignity appropriate to each state position held in his lifetime. When they arrive at the rostra, they all sit in a row on ivory thrones. There is no finer nor ennobling spectacle for a young man who esteems fame and virtue – especially to see these images of men well known for excellence altogether as though living and breathing. What spectacle would seem finer than this?[67]

Polybius' narrative places emphasis on the procession from the home to the Forum for the eulogy and passes over subsequent elements of funerals such as the burial and customary ceremonies. Theatricality pervades the procession from the appearance of the deceased, who seems to have been animated since his lying-in-state ceremony, if he rarely leaves the house prostrate but is carried sometimes upright (implying standing at other times?) to the assembly of his ancestors in the Forum, who take seats of honour near the rostra and compete for the attention of the mourners. The urban crowd that viewed the procession and events in the Forum formed a larger layer of spectators whose participation reinforced and validated the status of the deceased.

The animation of ancestors through the wearing of *imagines* by members of the family who play-act contributes to a spectacle that serves a didactic purpose in which the dead mingle with the living. In other sources, actors sometimes play dead, as in the case of Vespasian who was imitated by a mime actor who parodied the Emperor's gait.[68] The collective identity of famous ancestors is emphasized in a public (and very expensive) ceremony that provides an opportunity to advertise the accomplishments of the deceased as it simultaneously advertises the prestige of the family. Funeral processions share many of these elements with a military triumph in which a victorious general rode through the streets of Rome on a ceremonial route amidst representations of his military victory such as booty, placards, and hostages before the populace that served as audience to the spectacle.[69]

At the funeral of Julius Caesar in 44 BCE, a wax effigy complete with bloody stab wounds was displayed and rotated like a stage device above Caesar's body that was lying covered on a bier.[70] The effigy represented Caesar at the time of his death but it did not serve as substitute for his actual body during the funeral. It was instrumental, however, in arousing sympathy. Mark Antony continued the theatricality of the funeral as he dramatically revealed Caesar's body following his eulogy. The funeral aroused such a feverish pitch of sympathy that the crowd rioted, carried off Caesar's body, first to the Capitoline and then back to the Forum, and performed an impromptu cremation near the Regia (not the Campus Martius where a pyre had been prepared) where a temple and altar to the deified Caesar were later constructed.

Like the funerals of aristocrats, imperial funerary rituals were expressions of grief and public displays of political and religious propaganda but cremation centred on apotheosis and the manipulation of images, in particular the display of *imagines* in the form of wax effigies. The funeral of the emperor Augustus in 14 CE was carefully orchestrated down to the staging of the arrival of his procession into the Forum. The emperor's actual body was covered during the procession but he was represented by several effigies that converged at his bier in the Forum from different directions: one made from wax and dressed in triumphal costume was carried from the palace, another of gold was carried from the Curia Julia and a third arrived in a triumphal chariot. Multiple wax effigies of Augustus served to magnify the presence of the actual emperor and emphasize his various civic and military roles and achievements as Princeps.

Full-body wax effigies were later used for imperial funerals to serve as a substitute body when an emperor died and his remains had been disposed of outside of Rome.[71] The symbolic value of this *funus imaginarium* was immense: to give the populace of Rome an effigy onto which to project their grief in a public ceremony that demarcated one emperor's rule from another. The realistic appearance of the effigy and its treatment contributed to the theatricality of an event that was intended to symbolize the actual funeral of a real corpse.

The funeral ceremony of Pertinax in 193 CE for example, is remarkable for the 'life-like' appearance and role played by the effigy in sustaining the illusion of an actual corpse.[72] Prior to cremation on a tiered pyre, the effigy was dressed in triumphal clothing and displayed on a bier. A boy fanned the 'corpse' with peacock feathers to keep the flies away as though Pertinax were asleep. Septimius Severus planned Pertinax' funeral and as fate would have it, a *funus imaginarium* was held for him in 211 CE since he had died in York. A wax effigy of the Emperor was laid out in state in Rome and depicted with a sick face to resemble his appearance at time of death.[73] This 'realistic' depiction erased the distance between York and Rome by presenting the Emperor as newly deceased, as he would have looked had he died in Rome. The visible signs of illness provided greater contrast to the cremation ceremony on a tiered pyre that advertised Severus' apotheosis.[74]

The holding of symbolic funerals to mark the death of a head of state extends to President George Washington. As Washington's body lay in state in Mount Vernon, simultaneous funerals with empty coffins were taking place across the US Symbolic funerals with empty coffins are different from effigies serving as substitutes for the corpses of emperors, but they indicate the public's need to mourn the passing of a national figure in a personal way within a public ritual context.[75] Mock funerals of Washington continue today. On the bicentennial anniversary of his death, actors reenacted Washington's funeral at his home in Mount Vernon.

Funerals for public figures continue to attract a wide audience that turns a normally intimate service, whether religious or secular, into a public event that may be televised to reach millions of people. In addition to the funeral of President John F. Kennedy, recent high-profile funerals attracted worldwide attention. The funeral of Princess Diana is unique since the original plans for a private funeral were changed due to the public demands for a state funeral that were as much a need to mourn her death collectively as they were a way to right a wrong in the perceived indifference of Queen Elizabeth II to Princess Diana's status as the 'People's Princess'. Millions watched the media coverage of the cortège that featured the young Prince William and Prince Harry walking behind their mother's coffin. The audience for the funeral of Pope John Paul II was also a worldwide media event. The length of the Pope's papacy and his extensive travels contributed to the international grief experienced by his death, but the media coverage also attracted viewers who had not witnessed a papal funeral in decades and who were anticipating the Vatican rituals that accompanied the election of his successor.

In modern funerals, walking the cortège is more common in Europe and the Middle East rather than in North America due to cultural differences and the proximity between the cemetery and the funeral home or place of religious service.[76] The carrying of photographs of the deceased or placards in processions that pass through streets filled with people who may pause to watch approximates the effect of carrying and viewing ancestor images through the streets of ancient Rome. Musical instruments, including bagpipes, may be played to accompany the processions of political dignitaries, fallen servicepeople, or members of the military.

When not accompanied in a cortège, many modes of travel are available for the conveyance of the deceased. As with the shipping of cremated remains (Chapter II), the deceased may also travel by airplane to a place of disposal and stops may include airport terminals or the post office. For funerals in which the coffin is conveyed by a hearse, it may be taken directly from the funeral home to the place of disposal, if the deceased is not cremated on site; or to multiple locations from the funeral home to a religious service and then conveyed to the place of disposal, whether for cremation or inhumation.[77] Family members may follow in a limousine, with the black vehicles comprising the motorcade replacing the dark clothing worn by mourners walking the cortège. A reversal of the walked cortège or motorcade is found in 'drive-thru' funeral homes in the US where mourners pay their respects from their cars as though stopping at a drive-thru fast food restaurant, bank, or pharmacy.

New Orleans jazz funerals give more of a sense of the spectacle and sounds of Roman funeral processions. The dead are on parade in a dynamic and festive atmosphere that has more in common with Mardi Gras celebrations than traditional sombre funeral cortèges. The body of the deceased is conveyed in a hearse or carriage that may be glass sided or decorated with pictures of the deceased surrounded by mourners who walk alongside. Normally held for musicians and carnival krewes and organized and performed by fellow musicians who form part of the procession and play horns and drums that become progressively more upbeat once the deceased is buried. 'When the Saints Go Marching In' is typically played on the way to the cemetery as a dirge but a 'hot' or lively 'Dixieland' version is played on the way back from the cemetery. Younger musicians are substituting hip-hop songs.

Jazz legend Ernie K-Doe's funeral stands out from the jazz funerals of other musicians.[78] An effigy of K-Doe made from a department store mannequin and dressed in his performance outfit and a Louis XIV wig was placed on the seat of the horsedrawn carriage that conveyed his coffin to the cemetery. In a semiotic variation of a Roman funeral in which portraits of dead ancestors were carried in procession or worn by actors, the effigy of K-Doe represents the dead transporting the dead. The procession of thousands was compared to a Mardi Gras parade. After the funeral, his widow Antoinette K-Doe dedicated his club 'The Mother-in-Law Lounge' as a shrine to him and placed the effigy on a throne. The effigy was removed for Mardi Gras and rode in Antoinette's Baby Dolls' Krewe of Muses float in another example of the reciprocity between a jazz funeral and Mardi Gras parade. The effigy was also brought to Ernie's tomb on All Souls' Day and sat next to Antoinette, who served gumbo and soft drinks to guests (Chapter IV). The effigy would perform at another funeral: at Antoinette K-Doe's funeral, the effigy of Ernie was placed on the seat of the mule-drawn carriage that conveyed her coffin to the cemetery.[79]

This chapter examined how modern funerary practices, from preparing a corpse for visitation to the events leading up to disposal, share ancient strategies for avoiding contact with death while preserving the identity of the dead from the wake to the procession. Ongoing social relationships result from the restoration and perpetuation of the deceased's identity. The wake may be the first place in which this transformation is experienced, but the reintegration of the dead continues at the place of burial and through commemoration. The inherent theatricality of displaying the dead turns the deceased into an actor and the mourner into an audience. Chapter II examines shared strategies for disposal in the (re)locating of the dead physically and figuratively among the living, and the impact of death on the urban, suburban, and rural landscapes: how the dead and their burial monuments and containers maintain the identities of the dead and (re)define their surroundings.

CHAPTER II

DISPOSAL

'Another sifting of the remains is cruel and inhumane,' said Talat Hamdani. Her son, a police cadet, died on September 11. 'Sifting the remains will not provide the victims' families closure. On the contrary, it will only cause more pain by reopening their wound and it will inject a feeling of revenge once again in the veins of our nation.'[1]

A renewed effort to sift the soil removed from the World Trade Center site since 2007 is dividing the victims' families: while some want the search for remains to continue in order to provide closure, others like Talat Hamdani do not.[2] For Ginny Bauer, who lost her husband David, the issue is whether the remains represent her husband who survives whole in spirit, 'My husband and so many other people who perished that day, their remains could be anywhere,' she said. 'It's not who they are, it doesn't represent them. Their spirit is with us.' So far, of the 21,744 remains uncovered in previous sifting operations, 59% have been identified or 1616 out of the 2749 victims.

The varying reactions of the victims' families towards the recovery of remains reflect the extraordinary circumstances surrounding the deaths of the victims. For victims whose bodies were recovered, the temporary burial under the debris was followed by a secondary disposal whether cremation or inhumation. For those victims whose remains disappeared at the moment when the towers were destroyed, however, the site of death, Ground Zero, is also the site of disposal in a tragic fusion of death and cremation, whether the remains were buried amidst the debris or were scattered in lower Manhattan. As the site of disposal, the site is sacred ground just as the Fresh Kills Landfill where remains mixed with debris were brought and are again being sifted. For victims' families, the multiple burials and exhumations of the remains has increased the sites of death and commemoration as they have occasioned repeat and prolonged mourning.[3] This chapter focuses on the disposal of the dead from cremation to inhumation, including secondary disposal, exhumation and reburial, and sky burials.

Modern cremation and other disposal practices share similarities with those of ancient Greece and Rome in the variety of disposal methods but with notable exceptions that reflect modern cultural and religious diversity. The reinstitution of cremation in Europe is of itself an important part of the dialogue between ancients and moderns as ancient methods were relearned and (re)presented to the public as Neoclassical referents. Recently, economic factors are changing traditional disposal methods within families. As with funerals, the internet is changing how disposal is presented and viewed by a wider audience. Burials, committal ceremonies, and secondary disposal offer traditional and innovative options to dispose of the dead with varying participatory roles of survivors.

Cremation

In the West, the decision whether to bury or cremate is one of choice. A cremation may follow a wake or take place without any kind of ceremony such as in the case of cadavers donated to science, or a preference based on personal choice or cost. Research facilities, for example, dispose of cadavers and body parts collectively without any funeral rites. Since donors are aware that their remains will be disposed in this way, personal choice motivates their decisions. Cremation providers also offer no-frills options for those seeking a cremation without religious, ritual, or social elements. These 'direct cremations' are performed without visitation or a funeral service, with a simple coffin that may be made out of cardboard or plywood, and the cremated remains are returned to family members in a plastic bag or cardboard box.

By the end of the twentieth century, the majority of people opting for cremations in North America were from the upper classes suggesting cultural reasons rather than economic factors for the increase in cremations.[4] Economic status, however, may not fully take into account other cultural reasons, such as religion, the AIDS epidemic, and environmentalism, for the increase over the second half of the twentieth century. A variety of cultural reasons accounts for a similar rise in the number of cremations performed in the UK over the same period.[5] Overlapping cultural reasons behind the decision to cremate, however, make the application and prioritising of labels difficult. The same holds true when assessing the cultural reasons not to cremate. The apprehension among African Americans to cremate, for example, may not be due to religious or economic factors.

Religion may be a factor behind the increase in the number of cremations performed. Following Pope Paul VI's lifting of the 100-year-old ban against cremation in 1963, Catholics who traditionally practised inhumation burials may now choose cremation as a means of disposal. Immigrants from East Asia whose traditional religious beliefs require cremation funerals may also be contributing to the increase in cremations. The growing secularism in the West, however, provides another perspective of the influence that religion may exert on the growing number of cremations. Atheists may turn to cremation as a secular funeral option but their decisions may be based on social factors rather than religious ones.

Social factors behind the increase in cremations are part of larger cultural developments, such as the AIDS crisis for which cremations elicited personal and public responses: a way to dispose of the ravaged bodies of victims but also ways by which to minimize the perceived threat of the disease to public health.[6] Environmentalists are increasingly choosing cremation over inhumation as a 'green' choice and a scattering ceremony for conservation and spiritual reasons: to preserve land and to nourish it with their scattered remains. (See below and Chapter III for other green burial options). In some cases, the scarcity of burial land in urban centres may make the choice of cremation less about environmentalism or spirituality than about necessity.[7]

Recently, there has been a shift in the cremation paradigm with economic rather than cultural factors leading to an increase in the number of cremations performed in North America: the high costs of funerals and inhumation burials, high unemployment rates, and lost or drastically reduced retirement savings as a result of the economic recession that began in 2007.[8] The shift away from traditional inhumation due to economic reasons may indicate a temporary change forced on the poor or one that might have a lasting effect, as cremations become more popular and prevalent within families. Visits to the cemetery may require going to different areas depending on how family members are disposed.

Cost-saving funeral services and options are tailored to this financially strapped demographic. Internet and highway traffic are targeted: in addition to websites and advertisements for low-cost cremation services (a keyword search for 'low-cost cremations' brings up a large number of sites), billboard advertisements for cremations vie for the attention of motorists driving past billboards for motels and fast food restaurants. A billboard for Metro Funeral Services and Crematory Inc., along Highway 78 in the state of Georgia, for example, advertises a $695.00 cremation all-inclusive. Such marketing tactics are a change from the traditional discreet approach of waiting for (inevitable) funeral business but the information may be useful for individuals planning their own funerals or the funerals of others concerned about costs. The use of less expensive wood for coffins, such as pine rather than oak, as well as cardboard, is further reducing the cost of cremations.[9]

Staging cremations

In the West, cremations are performed indoors at municipal or state-approved facilities and usually out of sight of mourners. The separation of the memorials from the process of disposal replaces the ritual involvement of mourners with an institution-based technician who offers a commercial service. The lack of involvement also implies lack of oversight on the part of mourners that creates two distinct phases in modern cremations that occur in two distinct locations:

> Most crematoria and cemeteries, or 'crems' and 'cems' as they are commonly known within the death industry, are found on the outskirts of towns and cities. Generally offering ample parking and generous opening hours, these are accessible sites that may be pleasant to visit. A striking feature of a crematorium in particular is the strong delineation between public, 'front stage', area and private, 'backstage', work sites (Goffman 1959). The areas for public use are the churchy waiting rooms, the committal chapels, the chapels of remembrance and commemorative gardens. Backstage are the office, the stark cremator anterooms (which hold coffins until a cremator is free) the busy cremating room, and the room in which the 'cremains', as they are called, are ground up before being put into urns. The change in décor between front stage and backstage is as absolute as could be found in any theatre.[10]

The viewing of cremations as stage events extends the inherent theatricality of wakes to cremations through the liminality of the curtain that demarcates the stage from the backstage. The theatricalised stage presents the deceased as an actor playing a role before a grieving audience on a stage set with props. The dramatic illusion ends the theatrical role-playing once the deceased is moved behind the stage curtain out of view from the public. Backstage, the deceased resume their actual identity but even this is negotiable since their embalmed body is a semblance of its former self that will soon undergo its next transformation into ashes. The stage, meanwhile, awaits the next body whose display before a new audience will reprise the same role that was played by the previous body in a restaging of the same drama.

The internet is altering the traditional physical separation between visitation and cremation and extending the theatre metaphor to change the dramatic focus from the stage to the backstage. The webcasting of visitations for mourners unable to attend the funeral, with cameras installed in the cremating room, turns the formerly private activities of cremators backstage into reality show presentations or 'behind-the-scenes' features in real time to online viewers. The Cremation-Cam documents the cremation for family members who may want to be involved in this stage of the disposal but they may also want to monitor what actually happens during a cremation to allay fears that the body of the deceased was not cremated but sold to body harvesters or that the remains of the deceased were mixed with those of someone else or even an animal.[11] Real-life documentaries are also a source of entertainment: presentations of actual cremations on YouTube further blur the distinction between participating in a webcast funeral as a mourner and viewing it for entertainment as an emotionally detached audience member.

Revealing what happens behind the curtain to a corpse during cremation also shines a spotlight on the 'out of view' activities of the cremator. A search for cremations under Google images reveals several photographs of in-progress cremations, including a series of photographs of cremator Rick Kraus, Vice-President of Premiere Transport Crematory Service standing in the crematory freezer in front of bodies stored in cardboard boxes.[12] The final photograph shows Kraus packaging a box of remains on his crowded desk only inches away from a pack of cigarettes and a full ashtray. What may be of ritual and emotional concern to families may be a source of banal workplace repetition to the cremator.

The use of illusion and allusion is not new to the cremation industry and early examples of crematoria and columbaria allude to Classical funerary ritual and temple architecture to imply a tradition of cremation going back to antiquity, even though the dead were cremated outdoors in antiquity. The late nineteenth century saw a proliferation of crematoria in Europe and North America that used Classical and Romanesque architecture. Crematoria in Northern Italy were among the first in Europe. The Classical allusions of their names as temples and architectural designs in the Neoclassical style made allusions to ancient Rome explicit. The Classical tradition and the grandeur of the architecture challenged the authority and opposition of the Catholic Church. The Tempio Crematorio in Milan dates to 1880 – its current appearance and configuration is in the severe Greek Doric style and flanked by columbaria.[13] The Tempio Crematorio in Turin, in the Greek Doric style, followed in 1887 and soon after, the Tempio Crematorio at Staglieno Cemetery in Genoa in the Neoclassical style with a roof topped by a flaming urn [**Fig. 3**]. The Tempio complements the cemetery's Pantheon or Capella dei Suffragi whose design is based on the Pantheon in Rome. In Germany, one of the first crematoria was the Heidelberg Crematorium that was built in the Roman Doric style. The Crematorium at the Père Lachaise Cemetery in Paris, built in 1889 in a neo-Byzantine style, only two years after cremation was legalised in France, was surrounded by columbaria and originally had three halls, each with a furnace in the shape of a sarcophagus that allowed viewing of the cremation by family members.

The first crematorium in London, the Golders Green Crematorium built in 1902, used Lombard-Romanesque architecture to promote a modern

Fig. 3. Tempio Crematorio. Staglieno Cemetery, Genoa.

form of death ritual through historicising architecture. The Romanesque style was sufficiently ecclesiastical for the religious to feel comfortable about the practice and it implied a tradition of cremation that downplayed or disguised the newness of the practice to a wary public.[14] The landscaped setting of the Golders Green Crematorium, unconnected with a previous burial ground, contributed to the aesthetic programme but it also served a practical function: mourners would enter through one door of the facility and then exit through a door to the garden allowing for the successive flow of mourners.

American examples of early crematorium and columbarium architecture also rely on quotations to Classical antiquity. The San Francisco Columbarium, formerly part of the Odd Fellows' Cemetery, now called the Neptune Society Crematorium, is a freestanding domed Neoclassical building built in 1898 by Bernard J. S. Cahill. It is the only facility that was allowed to remain open for burials after a 1930s edict that mandated the closure and removal of cemeteries within city limits. Many of the urns and containers of various styles are visible in the niches (8,500) that line the rotunda, hallways, and rooms named after mythological winds on the ground floor or constellations on the first floor. The second and third floors are less ornate in design. This non-denominational columbarium, owned and operated by the Neptune Society of Northern California, still has space available and welcomes clients on their website to secure their 'niche in history.'

The Chapel of the Chimes, formerly the California Memorial Crematorium and Columbarium, Oakland, CA, was originally built in 1902 in the Romanesque style. In 1928, architect Julia Morgan expanded the original building by adding several chapels, cloisters, gardens, and fountains to create a peaceful retreat. The Columbarium, evocative of ancient Roman columbaria, is famous for its irregular shaped niches, some with book-shaped urns, which suggest the relaxing interior of a library, rather than a cemetery.

Modern crematoria, with a long history of providing cremation services in the West, no longer need to emphasize tradition through architecture.

The reverse may be true: that modern-looking cremation facilities advertise the latest technologies and customers may place more trust in modern
efficiency than traditional and by extension, out-of-date evocations. Enclosed
columbaria remain popular but recent modern designs mark a shift from
Classical quotations. Open-air columbaria at modern cemeteries are also
prevalent as cremation burials become integrated with the landscape of a
cemetery. Although above ground, these enclosed niches bridge inhumation burial and enclosed columbaria. This is especially the case when incorporated into the hardscape of a cemetery, such as the Arlington National
Cemetery Columbarium, whose vaults form part of a walled garden that
demarcates yet occupies space within the larger cemetery. Marble or granite
facing conceals cremation containers that replace classic-inspired urns and
cinerary sarcophagi.

Ancient cremations took place outdoors. The evidence for the Greek
Bronze Age is mostly literary such as the heroic cremations of Patroklos
and Hector in the *Iliad*. As with literary descriptions of funerals and ritual
mourning, these accounts became the source of a literary trope in subsequent Greek and Latin epic, especially elements such as the gathering of
timber, magnificent pyre offerings including human sacrifice, military
displays, ritual mourning, and the gathering of cremated remains for burial.[15]
Cremations were practised contemporaneously with inhumations from the
Archaic to the Christian periods.[16] The Greek Orthodox Church still does
not allow cremations.

In ancient Rome, cremations were practised alongside inhumation burials
in the early Iron Age and continued through to the Christian period.
Cremations were held outside of the city as prescribed by the Twelve Tables.
Cremations were performed by a professional (*ustor*) and could take place
at a designated area within a necropolis and the remains buried elsewhere
or at the site of burial in which case the ditch that had been dug for the
cremation was filled in and marked (*bustum*). Like funeral elements prior
to cremation or burial, variations depended on the status and wealth of the
deceased and his/her family. In the Imperial period, *ustrina,* multi-tiered
pyres for members of the Imperial family, were erected in the Campus

Martius (outside the *pomerium* of the City) that became part of a sacred precinct in honour of a deified emperor.[17]

Funeral rites continued at the place of cremation. According to the Elder Pliny, the eyes of the deceased were opened prior to lighting the pyre.[18] In a ritual called *ossilegium*, normally a finger was cut prior to cremation to be included for burial with cremated remains in a cinerary urn.[19] Varro claims that mourners would normally remain around the pyre until the body was consumed, the remains were then collected for burial, and the last word spoken (*ilicet*) that signalled that one could go (*ire licet*).[20]

Ancient cremations required ideal conditions: favourable weather, a sufficient burning temperature for a sufficient period of time, proper air flow beneath the pyre maintained through periodic stoking, the quenching of the pyre with a liquid to collect the remains, and even the absence of foul play such as partial cremations for the abuse of the corpse to deny the deceased a proper burial. An average cremation would have required most of a day, from dawn to dusk, to complete.[21] If the cremation was not performed under ideal conditions, the corpse would not be completely cremated and require further attention. By comparison, modern cremations take one to three hours in a cremation chamber (retort) at a temperature of 1,500 to 2,000 degrees Fahrenheit. After the body has been reduced, the remains are cooled for several hours before bone fragments are mechanically ground and placed in a container.

Even under ideal burning conditions, unforeseen circumstances could interrupt a cremation. The burning corpse of M. Lepidus was thrown from the pyre due to the intense heat that prevented those present from putting the body back on the pyre.[22] Impromptu cremations reflect sympathetic expressions of popular political sentiment. In the Roman Forum, P. Clodius' body was burned in the Curia by a mob sympathetic to him during his funeral in 52 BCE.[23] Magistrate benches were used as timber for the impromptu pyre that caused the Senate House (Curia Hostilia) to burn down. The impromptu cremation of Julius Caesar in the Forum in 44 BCE (Chapter I) by supporters also violated the prohibition against cremations in the City but it showed the power that a rioting mob could possess during a public ceremony, a lesson learned by Augustus, whose own funeral was brilliantly planned and executed.

Outdoor cremations continue in the East and Hindu, Sikh, Jain, and Buddhist ceremonies share many features with ancient Greek and Roman ritual.[24] After bodies are washed and anointed according to ritual, they are carried to a holy place and laid upon a pyre. The pyre in traditional Hindu cremations may be a structure built on land or on a platform that floats on water. After the body is cremated or even partially cremated, the remains are placed in the Ganges or brought to places that are sacred to ancestor worship. Orthodox and liberal practices vary in the location of the cremation. It is becoming increasingly common in large urban centres for a corpse to be cremated in a crematorium but for the ashes to be scattered and receive death rituals at a holy place. Should Western influences be read into this shift or do the pressures of urbanisation have a universal impact on traditional religious rites, whether cremation or inhumation?

An important recent ruling in the UK that legalises traditional Hindu open air funeral pyre cremations allows for this question to be reversed and consider the impact of Eastern funerary practices on the West. Newcastle City Council in February 2006 rejected British Hindu Davender Kumar Ghai's request (filed jointly with the Anglo Asian Friendship Society and legally supported by every major Hindu National organisation in Britain including a corpus of British Sikh gurdwaras) to be 'naturally cremated in a sacrament of fire.'[25] The request sought a clarification to cremation laws stemming from the cremation of Rajpal Mehat in a field in Northumberland in 2006 that was permitted by Northumbria Police and not prosecuted by the Crown Prosecution Service. The decision was upheld by the High Court in May 2009 but in January 2010, the decision was reversed in the Court of Appeal.

Ghai's application for an open-air pyre was found to be in compliance with the Cremation Act 1902 whose aims,

... were to ensure that cremations were subject to uniform rules throughout the country, to enable the Secretary of State to regulate the manner and places in which cremations were carried out, to require a crematorium to be a building which was appropriately equipped, and to ensure that a crematorium was not located near homes or roads.

The ruling accepted Ghai's stipulation that his funeral pyre would be 'enclosed within a structure' to satisfy the building requirement of the Act (which it does not define). The Court of Appeal deliberately avoided defining 'building', but it did rule in its rejection of the narrow definition of a building as an 'enclosure of brick or stonework, covered in by a roof' in the context of cremations that Ghai's 'structure' would be in conformity of the Act. The natural cremation structures in Gibraltar and Ceuta served as comparative models: 'They demonstrate that such cremations occur within a structure which is substantial in its extent, solid in structure, and relatively permanent in nature.' The judgment of the Court of Appeal will have an impact on the practice of Hindu funerals in the UK. Will Hindus alter the 100-year funeral traditions in the UK that adapted and fused traditional practices to conform to the Cremation Act 1902 and British funeral customs? To what extent will open-air funeral pyre 'structures' redefine the architecture of crematoria and the landscape of Britain?

The Natural Death Centre claims to receive over 2,500 calls from the general public for natural cremations and argues that interest in them is not limited to Hindus: 'This challenge by Davender Ghai and the Anglo Asian Friendship Society was inevitable, but the fact that it was brought by a British Hindu is not; it could have come from any corner of the country, and any part of our society.' British acceptance of natural cremations as an extension of natural burials speaks to the growing popularity of non-institutional funerals in favour of those with personal spiritual and environmental meaning.[26]

Containing the dead

The storage of remains at home whether inside or in the garden for permanent placement or for temporary storage until scattering (see below) reflects how much has changed in attitudes towards cremation and living in proximity with the dead. No longer relegated to the periphery in suburban cemeteries, the dead may now occupy the city centre in their former homes, except for Catholics who must bury cremated remains in a cemetery. 'Keepsake' containers are designed as decorative urns for display in the home, rather than as out-of-sight storage vessels. Cremated remains may also be mixed with paint to create portraits of the deceased or a copy of their favourite painting. Portraits of pets made from cremated remains are becoming more prevalent. Keeping the dead in their former homes has long been a feature of African home burials that keep the inhumed rather than the cremated remains of family members in the home.[27] Collective burial in a cemetery is replaced by the collective housing of both living and dead family members.

Today, cremated remains may be stored in a variety of containers from urns and chests to a plastic bag in a cardboard box for temporary storage. Cremation urns are available for purchase at funeral homes, crematoria, or online retailers with seemingly endless choices of shape, size, colour, theme, and material, whether stone, metal, ceramic, glass, or wood to suit the identity of the deceased. On eBay, for example, over 4,900 items were listed under a 'cremation urn' search.[28] One can bid or purchase with a 'buy me now' option, new and even used antique urns that are often listed without provenance and described as 'acquired at an estate sale years ago.' These antique urns are sought after as decorative display items with Neoclassical or Victorian designs but there is no way of knowing whether these urns are also reused for the storage of remains.

The online retailer, www.memorials.com advertises 7,500 urn and container choices organised under headings such as Discount Urns, Marble Urns, Metal Urns, Ceramic Urns, Art Urns, Religious Urns, Urns for Two, Military and Veteran Urns, Nature, Sports, Hobby, and Infant and Children's Urns.[29] Among the themed designs are the 'King Arthur', 'Guinevere', and 'Lancelot' urns; 'Cowboy Boots' urns, 'Flying Home' with a bird in flight; garden animals such as 'Frog', 'Squirrel', 'Cat'; 'Shriners' in the shape of a fez; 'Pride Flag', 'Democratic' or 'Republican' Bronze urns, and recreations of famous religious art such as Michelangelo's 'La Pietà' and a detail of his 'The Creation of Adam' from the Sistine Chapel, showing God's finger about to animate Adam's. Among urn choices with a 'Classical' inspiration are the 'Pyramid', 'Sarcophagus', 'Column', 'Parthenon', 'Olympus', 'Zeus', 'Apollo', 'Athena', 'Vesta', 'Centaur', 'Grecian', 'Sparta Bronze', 'Carthage' and 'Roman' urns. (Self-) identification of the deceased with the choice of cremation urns ensures a container that, like a tombstone design or epitaph, captures their personality.

Etruscan and Roman cinerary chests, urns and pots/jars (*cinerarium, urna, oss(u)arium, olla*) come in a variety of shapes and sizes but they are not as equally diverse as their modern counterparts. These containers are small in scale for tomb, funerary altar or columbaria burial. Early Etruscan examples from the eighth to sixth centuries BCE include pots, some with helmet-shaped lids, Canopic urns in the shape of human figures seated in chairs or terracotta or bronze shaped huts.[30] The latter evoke houses – to modern eyes – like the so-called house tombs (Chapters III and IV) but their evocation of domestic architecture is more significant metaphorically than literally. Later traditional shapes of Etruscan cinerary chests were made of stone, alabaster, or terracotta, often with a reclining figure on the lid and a five-figure battle scene on the front of the chest; but other themes such as episodes from Greek mythology and banqueting are common as are plain chests with a simple decorative element.[31] Roman cinerary containers come in various materials and shapes, such as temple-shaped chests, pitched roof lids, decorative urns, and unique shapes that allude to the profession of the deceased, including trade equipment and items such as a breadbasket.[32]

Cremation and inhumation rites were practised contemporaneously among Etruscans with no discernable distinctions between geographic areas but in time, cremation prevailed in the northern and eastern areas with inhumation being more popular in the southern and western coastal areas of Etruria.[33] The use of full-sized Etruscan sarcophagi spanned centuries, from the archaic period to the second century BCE, and were for chamber tomb burial. Etruscan sarcophagi were made of nenfro (volcanic stone) or terracotta, and could be monochromatic or polychromatic, freestanding or placed on benches. Effigies of the deceased often recline on the lids of Etruscan cinerary urns and sarcophagi as though at a banquet and engaged in conversation (called *kline* style after the Greek word for a couch).[34] Often, the sarcophagi are decorated with images influenced by Greek iconography and it is sometimes difficult to relate the effigy to the reliefs depicted on the sarcophagus chest, especially when Greek myths are depicted or battle scenes for the burial of women.

An early example of an Etruscan sarcophagus comes from the Banditaccia Necropolis in Cerveteri (ancient Caere) – the sixth-century BCE Sarcophagus of the Married Couple now in the Villa Giulia, Rome. The couple reclines as though engaging in conversation. The stylized elements do not detract from the animated expressions and gestures of the couple. Among many examples of stone sarcophagi is the sarcophagus of Lars Pulena from Tarquinia, now at the National Archaeological Museum, Tarquinia, which dates to the early second century BCE. The deceased reclines on the lid of his sarcophagus holding a scroll that may list his achievements. Depicted on the front of the sarcophagus is Lars Pulena between two death demons (charuns) holding hammers to signify his successful passage to the Underworld. The effigy and the depiction of the deceased in the afterlife advertise his current activities, in contrast with his actual body inside the sarcophagus.

The British Museum contains the Hellenistic polychromatic sarcophagus of Seianti Hanunia Tlesnasa found at Poggio Cantarello (near Chiusi) and dates to about 150–140 BCE. The deceased reclines on a mattress and pillow, wearing a tunic, a purple embroidered cloak, and jewellery, and is depicted as though she is in the process of adjusting her cloak. The gesture may indicate her modesty (*pudicitia*) but the animated quality of the portrait suggests a social context for it – did she just arrive at a banquet and is settling into place or did her cloak fall from its place around her head because her conversation had become too animated and her hand gestures had moved it from its place? The lifelike effigy seems to perpetuate the identity and personality of the deceased within a dramatic visual narrative.

Etruscan cinerary urns are smaller in scale than full-body sarcophagi but they share many features: for men and women, made from similar materials,

Fig. 4. 'Alabaster Urn of the Ionic Kymation 1 Group' Museo Gregoriano Etrusco, Vatican Museums.

an effigy or pair of effigies is often on the lid with some sculptural decoration on the chest. A Hellenistic alabaster cinerary urn with an effigy of a woman reclining on the lid holding a fan, known as the 'Alabaster Urn of the Ionic Kymation 1 Group' (Cat. 13896) dates to the last quarter of the second century BCE and early first century BCE, is now in the Museo Gregoriano Etrusco at the Vatican Museums [**Fig. 4**]. The deceased also appears on the chest of the urn reclining on one elbow on a couch as she is on the lid surrounded by women, one of whom holds up a chest. The museum text describes the scene as an apparition or a funeral leave-taking but it is not clear whether the woman herself is depicted on her deathbed, or at a banquet, or if the women are visiting her urn following her cremation.

Like the depiction of Seianti Hanunia Tlesnasa, the effigy of the deceased seems to make eye contact with the viewer as though about to engage in conversation. The sarcophagus seems to capture a real moment in the life of the deceased and illustrates the lifelike appearance of these effigies. When placed in their original context, the effect of walking into a chamber tomb with sarcophagi/portraits facing the entrance/axis points, whether the main or a side chamber, would have been like walking into a banquet room and interrupting a dinner and conversation already in progress and which is perpetually being enjoyed by the tomb's inhabitants.

Not all reclining effigies on Etruscan sarcophagi lids, whether for inhumation or cremation burials, however, are depicted as though engaged in conversation. A sarcophagus found at Vulci that dates to the late fourth and early third century BCE made from nenfro and now in the Boston Museum of Fine Arts, depicts a couple sleeping on their sides and facing each other underneath a coverlet.[35] The couple embraces with a remarkable symmetry of their limbs and the folds of the coverlet. The chest of the sarcophagus depicts wedding and funeral ceremonies that suggest the husband died before his wife and is now leading her to the afterlife where their original marriage vows are exchanged again in the Underworld. Another example is the famous sarcophagus of the Dying Adonis in polychrome terracotta in the Museo Gregorio Etrusco in the Vatican Museums (Cat. 14147) that dates to the late third century BCE. The sculpture is remarkable in its sensuous details of the dying boy and its ability to allude to the untimely and universal nature of death. Since there is no place within the sarcophagus to contain cinerary urns, the monument may have been placed on top of a chest that bore the identity of the deceased.

The depiction of an effigy or a portrait of the deceased as asleep or lying in state assures the living of the peaceful rest of the dead. The sentiment is similar to the 'Here lies . . .' (*hic iacet*) epitaphs and the wish for the earth to lie light on the deceased (*terra levis tibi sit*) on tombstones that represent the dead as asleep (Chapter III). These effigies recall how the deceased last looked prior to burial/ disposal but in a way that simultaneously suggests that the deceased lies at perpetual peace. The sleeping metaphor perhaps consoles survivors who last saw the deceased lying in state but who now see the deceased sleeping peacefully. The depiction and the metaphor do not deny the fact of death but rather, encourage an ongoing social relationship with the dead person, who is literally buried inside the sarcophagus but lies figuratively alive on the lid. The sarcophagus affects the interpretation of the tomb itself that is not only the repository of the dead but also a figurative bedroom of the sleeping dead.

The theme is an enduring one beyond Etruscan funerary ritual to the modern era. Recumbent effigies on the lids of Roman sarcophagi and kline monuments evoke domestic scenes to evoke the reciprocity between the tomb and home as eternal houses for the dead. Examples are numerous and a few examples will illustrate the thematic and chronological variety. The kline monument of a Flavian Woman, c. 80 CE, now in the Cortile Ottagono, Vatican Museums, for example, depicts the deceased as Venus. She is propped up on one elbow with her face turned as though to make sure that she is recognized by the viewer. Neither her facial expressions nor her gestures, however, have the social quality of Etruscan portraits but the primary message may have been one of apotheosis signalled by her depiction as Venus.[36]

A married couple, personified as the Earth goddess Tellus and a river god, recline on the lid of a marble sarcophagus that dates to the Severan period (c. 220 CE) and is now at The Metropolitan Museum of Art, New York (Inv. 1993.11.1). The couple, depicted in full length, converse as though at a banquet. The husband, reclining in the pose of a river god and holding a water reed, looks into the face of his wife who, personified as Tellus, holds a garland and sheaves of wheat. The portrait of the wife was never finished suggesting that the husband pre-deceased her.

Medieval and Renaissance sarcophagi with effigies of the deceased lying in state or recumbent, often with hands clasped in prayer, are common in European churches whether placed in a chapel, within an aisle floor or wall, or part of a funeral monument that could include other elements such as a canopy, columns, or angels.[37] The Basilica of St. Peter in Rome, for example, contains funerary monuments of popes in various positions: supine, recumbent, enthroned or kneeling in prayer and represent an art historical survey of the theme. The Cathedral Basilica of Saint Denis in Paris contains seventy recumbent effigies and tombs of French royals, nobles, and prominent clerics. The most elaborate is the tomb of Louis XII and Anne de Bretagne that contains two sets of portraits: recumbent effigies within a canopy structure upon which the couple kneel in prayer. Westminster Abbey also contains an equally impressive collection of royal tombs that depict the deceased in effigy. The effigy of Queen Elizabeth I, for example, lies in state dressed in royal splendour. Her hands are not clasped in prayer, but rather hold symbols of her earthly power: a sceptre and an orb.

Examples from the Renaissance and Baroque in other churches are also notable. In Rome, the bronze effigy of Cardinal Pietro Foscari (c. 1485) by Giovanni di Stefano (formerly attributed to Vecchietta) in the Church of S. Maria del Popolo lies in state in the Cappella Costa dressed in his clerical vestments to spectacular angular effect. The placement of the effigy in the foreground of the Chapel gives the impression of a funeral in progress. The effigies of Angelo Cesi and his wife Francesca Carduli Cesi in the Cappella Cesi, S. Maria della Pace, recline, propped up by an elbow, atop sarcophagi on facing sides of the chapel. The chapel is decorated in an Egyptianizing manner including the sphinxes that serve as stands for the sarcophagi. Marble for the monument came from the ruins of the Temple of Jupiter Optimus Maximus on the Capitoline Hill. Other important monuments are the reclining funerary portraits of Salvestro Aldobrandini and Luisa Dati, the parents of Pope Clement VIII, in the Cappella Aldobrandini, S. Maria sopra Minerva by Giacomo della Porta (1600–1602). On opposite walls of the chapel, the Pope's mother reclines with a finger holding her place in the book that she has just stopped reading as though interrupted by the viewer but the Pope's father reclines on a pillow propped up with books and he seems to look beyond the viewer as though lost in thought.

The tomb of Cardinal Richelieu in the Church of the Sorbonne, begun in 1675, depicts the Cardinal dressed in his robes and covered by a flowing coverlet and supported by a female figure who helps to hold him up and another who mourns at his feet. The assisted death scene of the tomb was designed by François Girardon, who studied in Rome, and shows the influence of Gian Lorenzo Bernini's variations on the recumbent effigy, such as his sculpture of Beata Ludovica in S. Francesco a Ripa and his Ecstasy of St. Teresa in the Cornaro Chapel (c. 1647–50) in S. Maria della Vittoria. Rather than depicting the deceased lying in state, Bernini made them the onlookers in a theatre box viewing the spectacle of St. Teresa's ecstasy and the angel who pierces her. Bernini transforms the chapel into a tomb, turning it into a theatre space while the viewer looks at members of the Cornaro family as they view St. Teresa. The act of viewing, however, is participatory: the viewer joins the Cornaro family as they view ecstasy creating multiple viewing subjects and audiences. The theatricality of lying in state is transferred to the scene of ecstasy, with the deceased as onlookers.

The Neoclassical tomb of Queen Louise of Prussia in Charlottenburg Park, Berlin, is a conscious evocation of Classical antiquity that downplays the theatricality of the Baroque. Upon the death of his wife in 1810, King Frederick William III invited leading Neoclassical sculptors working in Rome (Thorvaldsen, Canova, and Rauch) to submit designs for a mausoleum that depicted the Queen in the form of Death as Eternal Sleep. He selected Rauch's design, which combines abstract classicism with portraiture to depict the Queen sleeping on a bed with arms folded and legs crossed as though taking an afternoon nap from which she could awaken at any moment. The tomb is at once a portrait and an allegory whose Neoclassical style places it in a timeless present.

In ancient Rome, the growing popularity of inhumation burial in the second century CE led to a decline in the use of cinerary chests and an increase in the use of full-length sarcophagi (made of marble, stone, lead, terracotta, or wood depending on one's budget) for burial in a mausoleum tomb or hypogeum (underground burial chamber). In the East, sarcophagi could be arranged to line a street. Roman sarcophagi share similarities with their Etruscan and Greek precursors, in terms of shape and the variety of decorative designs from plain to ornate, with magnificent examples surviving from the second to third century CE.[38] The lids often resemble gabled roofs and may come with friezes around the edge and theatre masks at the front corners. Those with full-length effigies of the deceased recline in the style of Etruscan *kline* type sarcophagi. The chests are rectangular in shape and could be sculpted on all four sides in the Greek manner but they were more often sculpted on three sides since the unfinished backs were not visible when placed in a niche (*arcosolium*) or backed against the wall of a tomb. Decorative motifs include: a panel of vertical wavy lines (called strigillated after the strigil, a scraper that was used to remove oil from the body) that could frame a central relief panel or medallion with a portrait of the deceased, garlands, and lion heads. More detailed thematic elements include allegories of the seasons, the sun and the moon, and Castor and Pollux to reflect the brief span of the day as a metaphor for life and the cycles of life and death, bucolic scenes, and upside-down torches to represent a life extinguished. The finest sarcophagi incorporate mythological narratives that focus on the suddenness of death, suffering, or even joyous occasions such as processions and successful passage to the afterlife. Varied themes include episodes from the Trojan War, the Labours of Theseus or Hercules, the Calydonian boar hunt, Dionysus and his followers, Aphrodite and Adonis, Selene and Endymion. Other subjects include biographical events from and features of the deceased's life such as military service, a profession, marriage, or pastimes.

Of the many examples of sarcophagi preserved in museums, some famous examples of mythological and military motifs will indicate the high level of artistry available to the wealthy. The Endymion marble sarcophagus at The Metropolitan Museum of Art, New York (47.100.4) c. 200–220 CE is magnificently carved in the shape of a trough or basin for the pressing of grapes.[39] The lid is decorated with ten vertical panels that surround an inscription dedicated to the deceased, a woman named Arria, including one that contains her portrait. On the panel front, Selene descends from her chariot and approaches Endymion asleep below a female figure who pours out a potion of immortality and holds poppies to symbolise eternal sleep. The imagery alludes to Selene's nightly visits to Endymion, the passion of which is echoed by Cupid and Psyche, who appear to the left of a seated old shepherd. Bucolic scenes and amoretti are framed by lion

heads with the figures of Helios and Selene at either end of the sarcophagus representing the rising and the setting of the sun. Pastoral scenes
continue on the back of the chest. The sarcophagus' emphasis on the eternal
cycle of love immortalises the marriage of Arria and her husband.

The Ludovisi Sarcophogus dates to the mid third century CE and is on
permanent display at the Palazzo Altemps, Rome. The intricately carved
chest that was discovered near the Porta Tiburtina in 1621 depicts a dense
battle between Romans and Barbarians. The quality (carved from a single
block of marble with sculptures on three sides) and dimensions (nine feet
wide, five feet high, and four and a half feet deep) make it unique.[40] The
general (sometimes identified as Erennius Etruscus, the son of the Emperor
Decius, but he may represent an unknown member of the elite) at the top
and centre of the battle is a young man on horseback who does not wear
a helmet. The battle is fierce as Roman soldiers, on foot and on horseback,
slaughter Germans who are distinguished by their clothing, long hair and
beards. The sarcophagus has its own history with war – the lid, which
showed barbarians in submission and a bust of a woman (identified as
Erennius' mother, Etruscilla), was destroyed in 1945 when it was on display
in Mainz, Germany.

Christian sarcophagi were also used for inhumation burial of the wealthy,
whether for burial in mausoleum-type tombs or the catacombs' burial
chambers, among the niches of the less wealthy that line the corridors. They
share many stylistic features with pagan sarcophagi, such as the inclusion
of sculptural reliefs but with Christian themes: episodes from the Old and
New Testament, such as Adam and Eve, the sacrifice of Isaac, and the resurrection of Lazarus. Portraits of the deceased are depicted in eulogistic and
consolatory contexts within the visual programme of the sarcophagus.[41]
Other scenes include the receiving of the law, pastoral scenes of the grape
harvest and/or with the Good Shepherd with his flock who carries a lamb
over his shoulders, or Christian iconography, including trees, flowing rivers,
fish, putti, and garlands. A fragment of a sarcophagus in the Museo Pio
Cristiano, Vatican Museums, that dates to c. 325–350 CE [**Fig. 5**], depicts
Christ in a boat with the Apostles rowing (Inv. 31594 ex 236). Christ is at

Fig. 5. 'Fragment of a Sarcophagus with Symbolic Boat' (Inv. 31594 ex 236).
Museo Pio Cristiano, Vatican Museums.

the head of the boat as helmsman facing John, Luke, and Mark (the section
with Matthew is missing).

An early symbol of Christianity is the triumphal *vexillum* or *anastasis*,
which is comprised of the cross and the Greek letters Chi Ro as the
Constantinian monogram for Christ's name within a garland. On either
side of the garland are two doves and two soldiers: one awake at Christ's
crucifixion and the other asleep at the tomb. The cross symbolizes Christ's
Easter victory, thus turning a symbol of defeat into one of military triumph
in one of the earliest iconographic representations of the Resurrection. The
casting of Christ as a victorious general celebrating a triumph alludes to
pagan Republican and Imperial Roman military triumphs and adds another
element to his portrayal as a teacher, shepherd, fisherman or helmsman.

The sarcophagus of Junius Bassus rivals the finest pagan sarcophagi and
is one of the earliest belonging to a prominent public figure.[42] Junius Bassus
was the *praefectus urbi* of Rome when he died in 359 CE. An inscription
identifies him and lauds his accomplishments and life events, including his
conversion to Christianity shortly before his death. The marble sarcophagus was placed in the St. Peter's Necropolis under the original Basilica and
rediscovered in 1597. It is now in the Museo Storico del Tesoro della
Basilica di San Pietro with a plaster copy in the Museo Pio Cristiano in
the Vatican Museums. No portrait of Bassus appears on the sarcophagus;

however, reliefs on three sides depict scenes from the Old and New Testament on the front and pastoral scenes on the sides. On the front, columns separate ten niches with five on each of two rows. The top row contains the Sacrifice of Isaac, the Judgment or Arrest of Peter, Christ enthroned with St. Peter and St. Paul on either side of him, and two panels devoted to the Trial of Christ by Pontius Pilate. The bottom row contains Job on the dunghill, Adam and Eve, Christ's entry into Jerusalem, Daniel in the lion's den, and the Arrest or Leading to Execution of St. Paul. Other biblical scenes appear in the spandrels above the bottom row, including the Baptism of Christ. The sides of the sarcophagus are decorated with pastoral scenes illustrating the Four Seasons with putti, including the wine harvest.

Unfortunately for the history of early Imperial Christian burials, Constantine's tomb does not survive. The tomb, including his porphyry sarcophagus, within the mausoleum of the Church of the Holy Apostles in Constantinople (active until the eleventh century CE for the burial of Byzantine emperors and Patriarchs) was destroyed in 1461 for the construction of the Fatih Camii mosque complex. The immense porphyry sarcophagi of his mother, St. Helena, and his daughter, Constantia (St. Constance), however, do survive since they were placed in Rome.[43] Both sarcophagi are currently on display in the Hall of the Greek Cross of the Museo Pio-Clementino, Vatican Museums.[44] St. Helena's sarcophagus depicts victorious Romans on horseback with barbarian prisoners and others lying in defeat; overhead on the lid, putti fly strewing a garland. The lid has angels at each of its corners. The military motif of the sarcophagus' decoration and its placement within an Imperial mausoleum may signal that St. Helena's mausoleum (Tor Pignattara) on Via Labicana and the sarcophagus were originally intended for the emperor Constantine before he chose Church of the Holy Apostles.[45]

Constantia's sarcophagus is devoted to the grape harvest with pastoral scenes of vines and putti making wine, also a ram and a peacock, whose associations with death and rebirth in the afterlife have pagan precedents.[46] On the side, three putti stand on top of a castellum that pours out wine. The sarcophagus matches the interior decoration of her round mausoleum on the Via Nomentana, Rome (the tile mosaics in the ambulatory vault match the pastoral scenes and figures on the sarcophagus). Unfortunately, the original dome artwork does not survive. The mausoleum was converted into the Church of S. Costanza that is a popular site today for weddings where couples exchange their vows only a few feet away from a copy of Constantia's sarcophagus.

The afterlife of Roman sarcophagi is interesting for what it reveals about later generations' attitudes and interactions with ancient death, in particular the (mis)treatment of remains that were removed to make the container available for a variety of uses, both expected and unexpected. Many were reused as burial containers and Roman Imperial sarcophagi suffered the same treatment as the containers of the less famous, including unknown Christian martyrs.[47] Tradition asserts that Hadrian's porphyry sarcophagus, for example, was taken from his mausoleum (present day Castel Sant' Angelo) and reused by Pope Innocent II as his own sarcophagus for his tomb in the Basilica of S. Giovanni in Laterano. A fire destroyed the sarcophagus in 1308. St. Helena's sarcophagus was reused by Pope Anastasius IV (1153–1154) and moved to the Basilica of S. Giovanni in Laterano (from Tor Pignattara on the Via Labicana) and from there it was moved to its present location in the Vatican Museums by Pope Pius VI.[48]

The Vatican Grottoes contain numerous ancient sarcophagi, pagan and Christian, reused for the burial of Popes. Hadrian IV (1154–1159), the only English Pope (born Nicholas Breakspear) is buried in a reused pagan sarcophagus. The chest contains a garland with a bucranium and rosettes with two Medusa heads on the lid. Pope Pius VI (1775–1799) is buried in a reused Christian sarcophagus. The chest is decorated with a cross in the centre panel that is flanked by two strigilled panels. The fragment of another sarcophagus (fourth century CE) with one of the earliest depictions of the Epiphany sits on top of the sarcophagus. Although he died in exile in France in 1799, his remains had been transferred to Rome in 1802 and were later placed in the sarcophagus in 1949 at the request of Pope Pius XII. Pope Marcellus II (1555) is also buried in a reused Christian sarcophagus that was found in the Vatican Necropolis during excavation for the construction of the new Basilica. In the centre panel of the chest, Christ stands on a rock holding a scroll of the new law. Four rivers flow beneath the rock and two men stand on either side of him. Two strigillated panels flank the centre panel but are themselves flanked at each end with men, who may be St. Peter and St. Paul, holding scrolls and looking towards Christ in the centre panel.

The Basilica of S. Lorenzo fuori le Mura, Rome contains the funerary monument of Cardinal Guglielmo Fieschi, the nephew of Pope Innocent IV, built in 1256, that consists of a pagan sarcophagus with a wedding scene that is incorporated into a medieval Christian tomb [**Fig. 6**]. Originally, the back wall of the monument was painted with a scene of Saints Eustace and Hippolytus presenting Cardinal Fieschi and Pope Innocent IV to an Enthroned Christ. The sarcophagus is covered by a canopy, painted blue and decorated with stars to signify Heaven and is supported by ancient columns. The canopy and sarcophagus composition was a popular medieval design for church tombs and other examples include kneeling angels on

Fig. 6. Funerary Monument of Cardinal Guglielmo Fieschi with Roman sarcophagus. S. Lorenzo fuori le Mura, Rome.

either side of a sarcophagus that may include an effigy.[49] The couple on the sarcophagus exchanges vows by clasping their right hands with the Seasons and a scene of a sacrifice. The lid contains theatre masks at the two front corners with the figures of Helios and Selene at either end representing the rising and the setting of the sun. The sarcophagus commemorates the wedding of the formerly entombed couple and may seem an odd choice for the burial of a religious official but the rite of marriage is contextualized within the cycles of nature and within this context the rite of burial serves as another example of the passage of time and the themes of death and renewal. The monument was rebuilt after the Basilica suffered damage in World War II.

Other sarcophagi survive because they had been reused or converted into church altars, fountain basins, or decorative friezes in uses that remove them from their funereal contexts. In Rome, well-known examples of sarcophagi reused as fountain basins include Bernini's fountain in front of the Church of Santa Sabina that incorporates an ancient theatre mask as the spout. Other examples include fountains in Palazzo Patrizi, Palazzo Mattei di Giove, and the Villa Borghese. In one infamous case of reuse, the remains of Pope Urban VI were removed from his marble sarcophagus for use as a basin to mix mortar in the construction of the dome of St. Peter's.[50] Other sarcophagi do not survive intact but the front of chests were removed and incorporated into walls as decorative frieze panels in palazzi or on the façades of buildings. The façade of San Matteo, Genoa, for example, contains a late Roman sarcophagus relief that depicts the Allegory of Autumn with its own interesting history of recycling. The sarcophagus was first reused for the burial of the Genovese admiral Lamba Doria (1245–1323) who had brought it to Genoa from Korcula, Dalmatia, before its incorporation into the church's façade.

Burials and secondary disposal

In Benjamin West's famous painting, 'Agrippina with ashes of Germanicus', the artist depicts an episode from the historian Tacitus' *Annals* (3.1) in which Agrippina disembarks from her ship in Brundisium carrying the urn that will ultimately be conveyed by a relay of officials to the Mausoleum of Augustus in Rome. The dramatic episode served as a politicization of the Emperor Tiberius' refusal to hold a funeral in Rome and as a substitution for an actual funeral cortège. The epic treatment surrounding the conveyance of the urn contrasts with the modern realities of shipping cremated remains, whether one personally transports cremated remains or entrusts shipment to funeral or delivery professionals, or cadavers to their place of disposal.[51]

The shipment of cadavers is usually left to professionals but recently, two women were arrested at an airline counter at John Lennon Airport in Liverpool, UK and charged on suspicion of smuggling a 91-year-old dead relative to Germany. Airport staff became suspicious of the man sitting in a wheelchair and wearing sunglasses and prevented the women from boarding.[52] It was later reported that even though the man had died of natural causes 12 hours prior to the flight's departure the women claimed that they thought he was asleep.[53]

In ancient Athens the deceased was conveyed to the cemetery before dawn for burials that normally took place on the third day after death with some combination of offerings such as a lock of hair, animal sacrifices, and libations (*choai*) at the grave. Solon forbade the sacrifice of an ox at the grave but smaller animals were acceptable, with offerings of flowers and fruit. A eulogy (*epitaphios logos*) may accompany the committal but it was forbidden by Solon's laws to speak ill of the dead in public (Plutarch, *Solon* 21.1–2: *ton tethnekota kakos agoreuein*). Grave goods from personal items to vases and containers were often buried with the deceased. Burial was followed by a ritual meal (*perideipnon*) with survivors around the hearth of the deceased's house that corresponds to modern repasts or luncheons that often follow burial ceremonies.[54] At the meal, mourners wore garlands and delivered eulogies. Food and drink offerings were made at the grave on subsequent occasions (Chapter IV).

In ancient Rome, for inhumation burials or if a burial took place at the site of cremation (*bustum*) with a mound, rather than collected for deposit in an urn, it was required, at a minimum, to be covered with a handful of earth. Cicero (*De legibus* 2.22.55–69) claims that it is not necessary to describe burial rites that are in practice but he does emphasise that a burial only qualifies as a site of legal and religious significance with the sacrifice of a pig (see Chapter III for practical considerations). Inhumation burials could be in a pit, a simple mound, burial in a mausoleum, hypogeum, whether inside a sarcophagus or interment in the floor or burial niche (*arcosolium*) in tombs once inhumation burial became more widely practised than cremation. Grave goods such as coins, cosmetics, jars, toys, and figurines could be buried with the dead. Following the offering of sacrifices and libations, family members would participate in a graveside meal (Chapter IV).

Modern burials take place during the day and the committal service may be religious or secular.[55] The sequence of events recalls the theatricality of the wake and procession: carrying of the coffin by pall-bearers to the grave, which may be lined with carpet and covered by awning in warmer climates; the lowering of the body with a mechanical device, and the various roles assumed by presiding official, funeral home staff, or band in the case of burials with military honours; and mourners, all of whom recall the theatrical setting and the inherent theatricality of visitation and/or cremation that accompanies the 'disappearance' of the body. The throwing of a handful of soil or flowers over the lowered coffin represents a symbolic burial since the cemetery burial crew may wait until the family leaves to fill in the hole and patch up the grass. Several weeks or months may pass before the grave becomes a 'completed site' that becomes figuratively associated with the identity of the deceased through an inscribed grave marker and perhaps statuary and flowers (Chapter IV). A meal or repast may be held at the home of a family member following the ceremony.[56]

Burial rituals may be repeated at cemeteries that practise exhumation and the reburial of remains, especially in Europe where space is limited. At Staglieno Cemetery, Genoa, for example, remains are removed from inhumation sites after 12 years and transferred to an ossuary with its own memorial marker. In Mexico, bodies may be buried on top of each other separated by a layer of cement until ground level is reached, at which point, with a priest present, the grave is dug up and any skeletal remains are placed in a bag. The bag is then placed at the lowest level of the grave and stacked burials recommence. In contrast to the easing of cremation rites in the Catholic Church, Greek Orthodox rites forbid cremation in favour of inhumation and a coffin that is not airtight to allow for rapid decomposition. The decomposition of the body is important for exhumation rites. In rural Greece, women in the deceased's family exhume the remains and collect bones that are then washed and kissed before being transferred to an ossuary for final burial.[57] It is interesting to note that these modern exhumation and committal rites are a repetition of burial rites and mourning that ancient Roman funerary laws sought to prohibit.

Secondary disposal following cremation offers another and more direct opportunity for final moments with the dead. While less prevalent in Europe, the UK and North America, the private nature of the rite makes the exact number difficult to document. The scattering of remains in the USA may be done by funeral professionals or by family members who may choose to keep the remains stored in the crematorium until they are ready to claim them.[58] Ashes may be scattered at a location with sentimental value to the deceased or their survivors but if the rite takes place at a cemetery, the location is documented, should family members choose to have their remains scattered in the exact spot.[59] Since the person scattering the ashes may choose the time and place within the guidelines of government regulations, the scattering of ashes offers the possibility of more intimate contact with the dead by survivors during the actual disposal than inhumation burial done by professionals and often completed after the family leaves.

Water committals are another form of secondary disposal following cremation that differs from the ceremonial ritual disposal of a cadaver at sea from a ship.[60] The rite is most often associated with Hindu scattering of ashes in the Ganges but it is also practised in North America with growing commercial and government regulatory interest.[61] As with the scattering of ashes on land, family members may choose a site of sentimental importance and use the same site for other family members. In 2008, for example, President Barack Obama scattered his grandmother's ashes off the coast of Lanai Lookout, Oahu, Hawaii at the same spot where he had scattered his mother's ashes in 1995. Temporary water-dissolvable and biodegradable containers are available for water committals.

Secondary disposal in the form of fireworks that contain cremated remains offers an opportunity for spectacle that turns the theatricality of a wake into actual entertainment for mourner-celebrants. In 2005, the cremated remains of Hunter S. Thompson, for example, were shot from a cannon as part of a light show. Unlike spectacular elements in ancient Rome that accompanied aristocratic funerals such as the *pompa*, the participation of mimes, and scenic/gladiatorial shows, the deceased is the source of entertainment. The launching of cremated remains into the sky as part of a fireworks display or into outer space aboard a rocket as in the case of Star Trek actor James Doohan, is an unexpected twist to traditional Tibetan or Native American sky burials in which a cadaver is left out in the open to decompose subject to the elements and animals.[62] Perhaps the most unexpected firing of human remains, however, is the placement of cremated remains into bullets that can be used for sport or hunting.[63] Other options for after-death metamorphoses include turning cremated remains (or the deceased's hair) into diamonds or a coral reef as part of a permanent environmental living legacy.[64]

The disposal of the deceased begins the next phase of the figurative transformation associated with the commemoration of the deceased and the location(s) identified with them from where they lived, where they died, and where their remains were placed. The location of the dead often most determines, however, how they will be memorialised and the extent to which survivors continue to engage in ongoing relationships with them. In the following chapter, the changing periphery of the dead is examined to consider how the literal and figurative boundaries between the living and the dead are negotiated. Commemoration, whether alluding to Classical antiquity or finding innovative expression, still points to the perennial need for the living to visit and remember the dead.

CHAPTER III

LOCATION AND COMMEMORATION

The scene is apocalyptic: bodies, by the thousands, being unceremoniously shovelled into mass graves. In the days since Haiti was rocked by a 7.0 earthquake, the country's shell-shocked leadership has been struggling with the grisly problem of what to do with its dead. This Saturday, Prime Minister Jean-Max Bellerive announced that the government – or what's left of it – had already consigned some 20,000 corpses to giant holes in the ground, making little or no discernible effort to identify the deceased, let alone notify the next of kin.[1]

The political associations of mass grave sites in the hills of Titanyen, outside of Port-au-Prince, with the Duvalier regime add a further stigma to the burials. Proper burials and the identification of the dead are important aspects of Haitian religion, in particular the voodoo belief that the living must remain connected with their dead who continue to live after death.[2] Like other cultures with strong traditions of ancestor worship, these mass grave sites compromise more than the dignity of the dead; they also threaten future communion between the living and the dead by eliminating a burial site unique to an individual.

In responses to disasters in which decisions to protect the safety and health of survivors must be made quickly, the mass burial of victims shares similarities with the mass burial of the indigent from antiquity to the Victorian era. Haste also affects commemoration: whereas a disaster response necessitates non-traditional and collective measures that remove one's individuality, it is similar to the traditional methods of disposing of the poor collectively who are associated with others in similar financial distress in sections of cemeteries such as paupers' graves and potter's fields. Collectivity and loss of identity affect the deceased and their survivors, who must find unique ways to commemorate the indistinguishable dead.

Not all mass burials, however, are occasioned by natural disasters. The victims of genocide suffer an inhumane and collective disposal that further reduces their dignity and associates them with the horrific circumstances and locations of their death. In the case of the Nazi concentration and extermination camps at Auschwitz, for example, the scene of incarceration, torture, and death is also the site of the mass cremations of the victims. Other sites of recent genocides such as Cambodia, Bosnia and Rwanda were selected for their remote location, making it difficult to find the unmarked mass burial sites and to identify the remains of the victims.

A grave is a social construct that derives physical and figurative meaning by the living: it marks where someone is buried and commemorated, but the monument and epitaph (or their absence) also serve in the (self-) identification of the deceased.[3] This includes political associations that may make the grave the focus of ideological attention, such as the grave of Rudolf Hess, which had become a neo-Nazi shrine before its destruction and the exhumation and cremation of his remains.[4]

Identification and commemoration of the dead was of vital importance in antiquity. The ancient Greek word for a tomb, *sema*, literally means a sign that communicates a meaning, and in the case of a grave, it also serves as a memorial (*mnema*) to commemorate the deceased.[5] The Roman Varro links the definition of memory (*memoria*) to the word for monument (*monimentum* or *monumentum*), since memory gives meaning to a monument and associates it with the identity and actions of a person.[6] The duality of a tomb's purpose extends to its chronological function in the present and in the past: to mark where remains are (now) located and to commemorate who that person was when alive. How someone is commemorated can further add to the identity of the deceased as a literal and figurative

Fig. 7. Grave Monument of Belinda Lee. Protestant Cemetery, Rome.

postscript to their former lives. As with any symbol or metaphor, the sign is often open to multiple simultaneous interpretations.

The place of burial and/or tomb, as a representation of the deceased, has a transformative effect on the landscape or burial setting that becomes associated with death and the identities of those buried there.[7] An epitaph in Greek found in Rome commemorates the burial of a wife in the court-yard of the house and how her death and monument transform the space: 'Therefore, I have set up your tomb in the courtyard, so that I might see you, although dead, in my own house, your sweet name, Messia, my wife I will remember always.'[8] The husband perpetuates Messia's memory and physical presence in the home for an ongoing social relationship with her.

In the Protestant Cemetery, Rome, two distinct graves communicate different meanings about the identification of the deceased and their relation to Classical and other classicizing monuments in the cemetery. The grave of Belinda Lee (1935–1961) consists of a fragment of a torso in a toga from a Roman statue [**Fig. 7**]. The statue stands on a base that contains only the first name of the deceased. The inside of the statue has been carved out to serve as a planter that currently holds a spider fern. The grave monument represents

Fig. 8. Grave Monument of Maria Luisa Montesano. Protestant Cemetery, Rome.

a conscious evocation of Classical antiquity. The use of a fragment of an ancient statue rather than a Neoclassical imitation of one, however, suggests a direct connection between the monument and the deceased with the past.

The grave monument of Maria Luisa Montesano (1882–1968) incorporates fragments of ancient architectural elements including funerary art and cinerary urn [**Fig. 8**]. Elements are reused and arranged around a brick core in unexpected ways: a column base is attached sideways and bears the epitaph, a capital is placed upside down at the base of the monument, and a cinerary urn sits on top of the monument that would normally be inside an ancient monument. The various elements allude to ancient funerary monuments but their seemingly haphazard arrangement signals a break from tradition to make a unique composition that references the ancient past and the reconstruction of ancient funerary monuments, such as those along the Via Appia Antica (see below).

In contrast, the Neorealist grave monument of architect Giuseppe Perugini (1914–2004) is in the form of a cube set akimbo that seems to defy gravity

Fig. 9. Grave Monument of Giuseppe Perugini. Protestant Cemetery, Rome.

[**Fig. 9**]. Perugini's grave is unique and its modern geometric design among Neoclassical grave monuments literally and figuratively stands out in the cemetery. The signature of the deceased on the cube in his own handwriting identifies the grave but it also turns the grave marker into a signed work of art that symbolizes the architect who transformed the site of his burial into a declaration of the immortality of his architecture.[9]

This chapter focuses on the location and commemoration of the dead: how the physical and figurative barriers between the living and the dead are negotiated through changing boundaries and meanings given to graves and epitaphs that (self-) identify the deceased. The periphery of death, traditionally defined by the location of cemeteries and monuments, is changing as the dead, no longer relegated to the suburbs, are increasing their presence in the urban landscape just as the environmental impact of their burials is decreasing the presence of memorials in favour of green burials. The landscape of the dead is also the landscape of the living who currently interact with the dead and who will, with their own monuments and burial choices, contribute to evolving periphery. The legacy of ancient death endures in Neoclassical and Victorian monuments that commemorate both the deceased and the mourner in relation to ancient Greeks and Romans. These once-popular monuments now serve as a contrast to modern forms of commemoration that find meaning in the individual rather than the historic past.

The dead on the periphery

Non-emergency burial decisions are based on many factors, and often where someone is buried indicates how they are commemorated.[10] Until recently, in the West, the dead were relegated to church burial grounds or to the periphery of cities and towns. The recent custom of keeping cremated remains in the home has blurred the physical and figurative distinction and division between the living and the dead. Living rooms that double as cemeteries, as it were, offer opportunities to keep loved ones close by, but to the unsuspecting, containers holding cremains may be confused with other decorative items, and become the unintentional target of burglary.[11]

Historically, the decision of where to locate or relocate the dead has been motivated by religious, secular, or hygienic reasons due to disease or population growth. In Paris, for example, in the late eighteenth century, tombs were moved to the (then) outskirts of the city, from cemeteries like Les Invalides, to establish new cemeteries and catacombs at a distance from the densely populated urban centre in imitation of the cemeteries of ancient Greece and Rome.[12] Ancient Rome further inspired the decision to reuse quarries as catacombs and bodies were moved out of crowded and disease-ridden church cemeteries into the new Paris catacombs.

The founding of the Père Lachaise cemetery by the City of Paris government was part of the movement to translate the dead from the cemeteries in the urban centre to the periphery of the city. To ease anxiety over the moving of the dead and to attract interest among the rich and famous for their own tombs, the planner Nicolas Frochot convinced authorities to relocate the remains and graves of Abélard and Héloïse, Molière, and La

Fontaine. The plan was successful and the cemetery began to attract people who paid high sums to be buried among such illustrious company. Neoclassical monuments made further connections with ancient Greece and Rome explicit and lent a sense of grandeur to the landscaped grounds.[13] Today, the cemetery attracts tourists who come to visit the graves of the famous, including those of Oscar Wilde and Jim Morrison.

The periphery between the living and the dead may be defined and delineated by the sea. The island of San Michele, also known as the Island of the Dead, was dedicated as Venice's cemetery in 1807, when under French control, to avoid unsanitary burials on the mainland. In 1836, the canal between San Michele and the island of San Cristoforo della Pace was filled in to enlarge the cemetery. The cemetery is still in use and special funeral gondolas transport the dead from the mainland to the island in a figurative evocation of the dead crossing the River Styx and the liminality between life and death and the living and the dead. The cemetery is a popular tourist destination and famous graves include those of Igor Stravinsky, Sergei Diaghilev, Ezra Pound, and Luigi Nono.

In North America, early memorial or cemetery parks were located away from urban centres as destinations whose landscaped grounds blended with their rural surroundings through evocations of Classical antiquity. Among the earliest are Mount Auburn Cemetery in Boston, MA (1831), the oldest land-scaped garden cemetery in the US, and Laurel Hill in Philadelphia, PA with its monumental gatehouse (1835) and Green-Wood Cemetery, Brooklyn, NY (1838). Forest Lawn Cemetery, Glendale, CA is unique. The layout of the cemetery was intended to deemphasize family and individual plots in favour of landscaped grounds. Statues inspired by ancient Greek and Roman, Renaissance, Baroque, and Neoclassical originals dot the landscape while the bronze markers are barely visible on the rolling hills. The grave monument of Walter and Beulah Overell, for example, is a reproduction of Gian Lorenzo Bernini's Daphne and Apollo [**Fig. 10**]. The mythological rape scene plays out among other scenes such as the 'Finding of Moses' and an exact replica of Michelangelo's 'David'. Copies of Michelangelo's other sculpture and a stained glass replica of Leonardo da Vinci's 'Last Supper' are located in the Great

Fig. 10. Grave Monument of Walter and Beulah Overell.
Forest Lawn Cemetery, Glendale, CA.

Mausoleum. Today, the cemetery contains a museum with other replicas of famous art such as Ghiberti's doors to the Florence Baptistery (Battistero di S. Giovanni) and a museum store for tourists who stroll the grounds and enter the Great Mausoleum to visit the graves of Hollywood celebrities.[14]

The Neoclassical landscaped cemetery park filled with famous statues of the kind that Cicero planned as a memorial for his daughter Tullia (*Ad Att.* 12.18.1) provided an opportunity for a romanticized or idealized recreation of the remains of ancient burials based on the 'pastoral' appearance of contemporary Rome in the eighteenth/nineteenth century, before the city was transformed into a modern capital following the unification of Italy. Looking to the past to make the contemporary landscape evoke both the original and ruined appearance of ancient cemeteries and monuments coincides with the modern family cult of the tomb. In Paris, as a reaction to the moving of the dead to the periphery, permanent homes and rights were sought for them.[15] Perhaps the quotation of antiquity gave a sense of permanence and an easing of the anxiety of family members who experienced the moving of dead family members and may have feared similar treatment of their own remains. The moving of the dead produced layers of imitation: the fact that in North America, burials in Neoclassical landscapes were not reburials, points to the imitation of European cities that were themselves recreating and emulating antiquity. The popularity of Neoclassical references produced a counter movement in Gothic and Neogothic cemeteries and grave monuments that appealed to those who sought indigenous references.

Contemporary refocus on the landscape as a burial space involves environmental considerations rather than aesthetic ones. Natural burials in green cemeteries cater to the eco-conscious corpse: the ecological impact and the benefits to the land that derive from natural burials are more important factors than incorporating memorials into the landscape.[16] Anonymous burials in unmarked graves, rather than a sign of indigence or a mass burial, put the focus on the environment rather than the deceased. This lack of identification and commemoration of those buried runs counter to the practice over millennia of planting flowers at the site of burial that is identified by a tomb and epitaph. The idea of nourishing the earth and flowers with one's remains appears in Greek and Latin epitaphs. The epitaph of the Freedwoman Flavia Nicopolis, dedicated by her husband with whom she was buried, for example, associates the deceased with the flowers at the site of burial:

O if the gods should grant my request
    that I see a new flower growing from your tomb
with a leafy branch or sweet smelling flower
either a rose or the purple hue of a violet,
so that should some passer-by walking at a slow pace
see these flowers, let him read this inscription and say to himself
    'This flower is the body of Flavia Nicopolis'.[17]

The flowers attract the attention of the passer-by who reads the epitaph and discovers that the deceased is the flower. Both acts are essential for commemoration and provide a contrast to the modern practice of natural burials whose benefits to the earth often outweigh concerns about the identification and commemoration of the deceased.

In urban centres with considerable population growth, once suburban cemeteries are now part of the urban fabric of cities as urban sprawl with office buildings, housing subdivisions, fast food restaurants, and strip malls absorbs once isolated or distant burial grounds. Mount Pleasant Cemetery in Toronto, Ontario, Canada, for example, was designed in 1876 as an idyllic oasis with lakes, fountains, and winding roads outside of the city, but today it is part of the urban centre.

If the dead increasingly share the (sub)urban space of the living, it is a reciprocal relationship, since the living cross the periphery into the territory of the dead to reach destinations surrounded by once distant cemeteries. These 'urban islands of the dead' seem like gated communities that are part of the urban fabric yet are not accessible to drive-through or pedestrian traffic. The cemetery gates function as literal and figurative boundaries between the living and the dead to those entering in order to visit graves, but in Cairo where the rural population is moving into the active cemetery Al Qarafa and taking up residence with family members and animals among the graves, the boundary is erased and the once City of the Dead is literally now a city of the dead and living.

Mediterranean cemeteries, on the edge of a city or town, maintain the traditional distance and separation between the living and the dead. The typical cemetery has high walls, iron gates, and tall cypress trees. Monumental proportions and decorative entrances that look like city gates are common to the cemeteries in larger cities, such as those at Campo Verano Cemetery, Rome. The Mediterranean-style Recoleta Cemetery, Buenos Aires, has an imposing Neoclassical entrance in the Doric style. The northern main gate of the Cementerio de Cristóbal Colón in Havana, Cuba, evokes a city gate in the form of a triumphal arch. Older walled cemeteries in North America share a similar appearance but with a mixture of conifer and deciduous trees that give the impression of a walled garden.

Space is at a premium in cemeteries and the walls that serve as boundaries to demarcate the area of the cemetery often perform a double duty and function as burial vaults which are incorporated into the interior side of the wall in ordered rows. Whether entering Staglieno Cemetery, Genoa or St. Louis Cemetery No.1, New Orleans, LA, for a North American example, one is literally surrounded by burial vaults, some located high off the ground, within steps of entering the gates. Due to the shortage of space, burial plots are reused in many European cemeteries. Remains are exhumed and translated to an ossuary after a prescribed period of time to make room for more recent burials. The (re) burials are consecutive, not contemporaneous.

The cemetery, as a social space, represents a microcosm that is increasingly as multicultural as society as a whole. Until relatively recently, however, many cemeteries had a history of exclusive/inclusive burials defined by religion, nationality, race, and social status. Within cemeteries, burials are often further defined and separated by religion, class, wealth, or age in the case of infants, creating peripheries within the periphery. The cemetery commonly described as the Protestant Cemetery, Rome [**Fig. 11**] is in fact called the non-Catholic Cemetery for Foreigners at Testaccio (Cimitero

Fig. 11. Protestant Cemetery, Rome with a view of the Tomb of Gaius Cestius and the Porta S. Paolo.

Acattolico per gli Stranieri al Testaccio). The name is exclusionary to distinguish it from Catholic cemeteries but it is not limited to just Protestants since the cemetery also contains Eastern Orthodox and Jewish burials. The cemetery is associated with the Grand Tour and is the final resting place of John Keats and Percy Bysshe Shelley. Neoclassical monuments, such as the Tomb of Lady Temple, with a relief of a Classical funeral procession, Greek steles, and copies of the sarcophagus of Lucius Cornelius Scipio Barbatus (consul 298 BCE) frame these imitative Neoclassical memorials in relation to their ancient precursors and unite the deceased as Classicizing foreigners.[18] In Florence, Italy, the English Cemetery (Cimitero degli Inglesi) in Piazzale Donatello, is dominated by English (and Protestant) burials due to the great number of English in Florence in the nineteenth century. The cemetery closed in 1877 when intramural burials were forbidden. A city boundary may also serve to demarcate burials along religious lines: in Toronto, Ontario, only members of the Catholic Church and the Church of England could be buried within city limits.

The recent opening of exclusive Muslim cemeteries in the West reflects a return to exclusive burials due to religious concerns associated with burials and visits to non-denominational cemeteries. It is important in Islamic law, for example, for burial plots to face east and for visitors not to step or sit on graves when visiting the graves of loved ones or to pray *jinaza* for them. The planning of most Western cemeteries with various burial orientations and rows of plots laid out so that visitors must step on the lawns planted over burials makes the observance of Islamic law difficult in non-Muslim cemeteries. In the Greater London area, the 'Gardens of Peace' is the largest Muslim cemetery in the UK. In the Detroit area of Michigan, where a large Muslim population resides, the opening of Muslim cemeteries such as the 'Islamic Memorial Gardens' in Westland, MI and the 'Garden of Peace' in Flint, MI, represents a shift in the US from burial in non-denominational cemeteries such as Roseland Park, Detroit where Muslim burials formerly took place.

Exceptional circumstances such as the outbreak of a disease or disaster or military service may unite, in the same cemetery, otherwise diverse burials. Cemeteries in Halifax, Nova Scotia, for example, contain the remains of many of those recovered from the Titanic.[19] Collectively, their deaths and tombs attract attention for their association with the sinking of the Titanic, perhaps at the expense of their individual identities and personal accomplishments.

Cemeteries for the burial and commemoration of veterans (re) unite men and women who served their country. Veterans' cemeteries may be in one's home country, such as Arlington National Cemetery, or the country of war, such as Flanders Field in Belgium, which permanently redefined the landscape in connection with WWI and reciprocally, the landscape with the dead: the poppies growing there are associated with the cemetery and are still used to commemorate the dead on Remembrance Day.[20] Veterans' cemeteries in other countries commemorate the dead in other wars. About seven miles outside of Florence, Italy, the American Cemetery and Memorial contains the burials of American soldiers who died in WWII in battles between Rome and the Alps following the capture of Rome in June 1944. The symbolism of burials extends to commemoration often associated with the expression 'lest we forget'.

Modern war memorials of either actual burials or cenotaphs, from the Greek words for empty (*kenos*) and grave (*taphos*) to signify an empty tomb, for the collective commemoration of the fallen, whether the Tomb of the Unknown Soldier or national memorials, like the WWII and Vietnam Memorials in Washington, D.C. or the National War Memorial in Ottawa, Canada, serve as tributes to heroism and service to the country. The marking of the actual place of battle or commemoration with an epitaph recalls the epitaph that marked the location of the Battle of Thermopylae (480 BCE) 'Stranger, tell the Spartans that we who lie here obeyed their orders.'[21] The landscape is permanently identified with a monument to the collective fallen as a reminder of their bravery to the living.

In early Imperial Rome, pagans, Christians, and Jews could choose burial associations, such as funeral clubs, that would keep them within a social group, but they were often buried in close association with each other due to the proximity of catacombs with pagan necropolises and roadside burials (elite and non-elite) outside of the city (see below for pagan burials in the catacombs of S. Sebastiano and St. Peter's Necropolis). Due to the blending of pagans, Christians, and Jews and the establishment of burial paradigms that influenced later European and North American (with English traditions) burial practices, the city of Rome is the main focus in following sections.

The ancient dead on the periphery

In ancient Greece, the necropolis was located outside the city, with tombs by the roadside. Collective burials located in distinct and defined areas outside the city contrast with some earlier Bronze Age burials, such as those at Mycenae in which royal tombs were located in a precinct within the city walls. As with many features of Greek culture, variations existed between city-states and regions. In Sparta, for example, the dead were buried within the city walls. Intramural burials removed the periphery between the living and the dead to create a city of 'living history' in which successive generations, living and deceased, shared the same urban space.

The Kerameikos cemetery in ancient Athens was located just outside the city wall and the main entrance to the agora on the northwest edge of the city. The cemetery, in continuous use from about 1100 to 200 BCE and again in the Roman period, contained a variety of tomb types and markers such as a mound, krater, grave marker (stele) that could be a simple slab or stylized pillar of stone or wood, painted funerary plaques, and monuments, including freestanding sculptures of young men (*kouroi*) and less frequently young women (*korai*) that were mostly used for votive offerings.[22] Not all of these types of burial markers are contemporaneous and legislation that affected the elements of funerals (Chapter I) also prescribed burials and the type and size of monuments.[23] The transition between the Archaic and the Classical Period saw the disappearance of stone stelai until their reemergence in the mid-fifth century BCE, when ordinary citizens, often depicted in a domestic setting, seem to equate their status as citizens to that of traditional aristocrats, who used funerary monuments and art to advertise their lineage and elite status.

Stylized sculpture gives a generic impression of the deceased and their

Fig. 12. Stele of Megakles. Accession Number 11.185a–d, f, g, x.
The Metropolitan Museum of Art, New York.

status within the polis, rather than a portrait, that is often reinforced by a
brief epitaph. The deceased, moreover, is shown as alive on relief sculpture
and the effect is one of a timeless present with the deceased still in it. The
stele of Megakles (c. 530 BCE), found in the Kerameikos Cemetery now
in the Metropolitan Museum of Art, New York, is just over 13 feet high,
and depicts a relief of a young man and a girl whose relationship is ambiguous
[**Fig. 12**]. The generic appearance of the boy and girl as they walk side by
side adds to the timeless quality of the relief as though they are still walking
at the present time. An apotropaic sphinx that sits on top of the stele still
guards the tomb in its new Museum context. The (restored) inscription on
the base reads: 'to Me[gakles], on his death, his father with his dear mother
set [me] up as a monument.'

On contemporaneous painted funerary plaques (c. 600–480 BCE),
however, the deceased is shown as dead in scenes of prothesis and ekphora.[24]
None of these plaques have been found *in situ* so it is impossible to say

whether the same tomb could have depictions of the deceased as alive in reliefs but dead on funerary plaques. What could be said, however, is that some tombs had reliefs depicting the deceased as alive and some had plaques that depicted the deceased as dead during the funerary rites that preceded burial (see Chapter IV). Visitors to the cemetery on the day of a funeral would be surrounded by depictions of the dead continuing to engage in everyday activities or dead being mourned and conveyed to the spot that now contains their remains.

In the Classical period, naiskos-style grave monuments depicted the deceased (and others) framed within a temple, in the round or in relief. The grave circle of the family of Koroibos contains three stelai, including the stele with the relief of a woman Hegeso, who is depicted seated within a naiskos before a servant girl who holds her jewellery box. Other stone naiskos tombs contain painted scenes, rather than relief sculpture. Painted stele become popular in the Hellenistic period and many fine examples survive from Egypt. At the end of the Classical period, stone sarcophagi placed in terraces that lined the high walls of the Kerameikos Cemetery became popular. Monuments were placed along the edges of the terraces rather than at the actual burial site, thus creating burial markers and commemorative monuments for the same person. Today, the cemetery is open to visitors and tourists who can walk among reconstructed and dilapidated tombs. The Kerameikos Museum displays kraters, vases, sculpture, and tomb monuments recovered from the cemetery.

The First Cemetery of Athens, Greece, opened in 1837 and was built behind the Temple of Olympian Zeus and the Panathinaiko Stadium. The central location of the cemetery and its proximity to ancient monuments lends it a Classical air that other cemeteries must imitate through Neoclassical design. The Neoclassical monuments, such as the Doric temple tomb of archaeologist Heinrich Schliemann, complement the setting. The cemetery is still active and includes the tombs of many famous Greek politicians and artists.

Like the Greeks, Etruscans located their necropolis outside of the city but their features were distinct. Etruscan cemeteries were usually rambling, rather than narrowly confined by a wall, and situated on hilltops or the slopes of hills. The area between the necropolis and the city served as a metaphorical abyss to separate the living from the dead. The Tarquinia Necropolis (also known as the Monterozzi Necropolis), for example, is five kilometres in length and one kilometre in width with underground burial chambers and is situated on a hill. The Necropolis contains 6,000 underground tombs that were cut into the rock (tufa), 200 of which are painted tombs including the famous Tomb of the Leopards (c. 480–470 BCE) that contains a convivial banquet scene of diners, musicians, and dancers. More modest grave markers include (*cippi*), a large or carved stone, such as the shape of a pinecone, or painted funeral plaques that were used only in Chiusi.[25]

The topography of an Etruscan necropolis is shared by recent examples: in addition to Staglieno Cemetery, Genoa, the Cimitero di Trespiano and the Cimitero delle Porte Sante that surrounds the Basilica of San Miniato al Monte overlook the historic city centre of Florence, Italy. The Cemetery of Montjuïc, Barcelona, Spain occupies a hillside whose Victorian monuments and mausolea are famous for their grieving angels. The Glasgow Necropolis, Glasgow, Scotland (inspired by Père-Lachaise cemetery in Paris) is located on the hill above Glasgow Cathedral and is reached by the 'Bridge of Sighs'. In the USA, pioneer cemeteries in the Old West were located on hillsides called boot hills, the monuments of which communicated the wealth and stability of towns.[26] With the growth of cities, boot hill cemeteries evolved into landscaped parks similar to those of eastern cities, such as Boston and Philadelphia.

In addition to underground burial chambers, the Etruscans buried their dead in tumulus tombs as at the Banditaccia Necropolis in Cerveteri (ancient Caere). Etruscan tumuli had circular retaining walls both cut from the living tufa and built up in masonry. Some of the mounds, however, are square in shape and are colloquially called 'dice'. The interior areas of the tombs (*hypogea*) were sunken and intended for multiple burials. Some tombs have several entrances to the various chambers, often with several rooms in each chamber emanating from the main room that one encounters first upon entering a tomb. The famous Tomb of the Reliefs (third century

BCE) imitates a Great Room with decorative columns, painted ceiling, and carved weapons and implements from daily life along the walls, which contain burial niches and platforms for sarcophagi. The tumulus design may have influenced the architecture of Augustus' and Hadrian's mausolea in Rome which infused the traditional form of Etruscan tombs with Hellenistic dynastic meaning through scale, construction during their life-time, and their designation as Imperial dynastic burial chambers next to *ustrina* precincts that commemorated the location of the emperor's crema-tion and dominated the (sub) urban landscape.[27]

Etruscan tombs were filled with sarcophagi, cinerary urns, and grave goods that suggest opulent banquets in progress, in particular in tombs with frescoes depicting banquets or those containing sarcophagi with portraits of the deceased reclining on the lid (see Chapter II). The magnifi-cent tomb of the Volumnii in Perugia, for example, contained seven cinerary urns with reclining effigies in the *hypogeum* that were arranged around the crypt of the tomb's founder Arnth Velimna and oriented to face the visitor upon entrance into the tomb as though a late arrival to the banquet already in progress.[28] D.H. Lawrence noted the festive, rather than sombre atmos-phere of Etruscan tombs that pervades tombs of the Hellenistic period, in his description of the frescoes in the Tomb of the Leopards in Tarquinia:

> The walls of the little tomb are a dance of real delight. The room seems inhabited still by Etruscans of the sixth century before Christ, a vivid, life-accepting people, who must have lived with real fullness. On come the dancers and the music-players, moving in a broad frieze towards the front wall of the tomb, the wall facing us as we enter from the dark stairs, and where the banquet is going on in all its glory. Above the banquet, in the gable angle, are the two spotted leopards, heraldically facing each other across a little tree. And the ceiling of rock has chequered slopes of red and black and yellow and blue squares, with a roof-beam painted with coloured circles, dark red and blue and yellow. So that all is colour, and we do not seem to be underground at all, but in some gay chamber of the past.[29]

In ancient Rome, burials were located outside the city walls in a variety of burial types: necropolis, mausolea, columbaria, catacombs, and tombs along the roads leading to/from the city. Burial within the walls, however, is attested in the archaic period in the Archaic Necropolis in the Roman Forum and later for the burial of children.[30] The construction of new city walls under the Emperor Aurelian (270–275 CE) at some distance from the original Servian walls meant that burials once located outside the Servian walls were now located within the Aurelianic walls, named after the Emperor Aurelian, such as the tombs along the Via Appia between the Porta Capena and the Porta Appia (S. Sebastiano). Intramural burials returned in the sixth/seventh century CE following the collapse of the city.[31] Since the walls demarcated the periphery of the dead, city gates served as literal and figurative barriers between living and the dead. Unlike the modern experience of driving by a suburban cemetery, ancient and medieval travellers (before their destruction) would enter and exit the city from tomb-lined roads and cemeteries.

Amidst the mausolea, cenotaphs, hypogea and monumental tombs of the elite (from so-called house tombs, temple tombs, towers, circular monuments, benches, and altars) that lined the roads were tombs and burial markers of various types and sizes of collective burial for the non-elites.[32] The poor, when not receiving a mass burial, could be buried in a trench (*fossa*) or under a mound of earth that was covered by a row or just two terra cotta roof tiles to form a roof or a simple cement vault.[33] Grave markers could take the form of an amphora vase, a *columella* (a stela made from native stone that could be shaped into a stylized head) or a *cippus* (similar to Etruscan stone markers). Pipes at the site of burial for grave offerings are common (Chapter IV). In catacombs and columbaria, niches were sealed with mortar and either a stone or terracotta plaque that could be used to identify the deceased but the name could also be painted below the niche. Both *cippi* and altars could be placed inside tombs, alongside sarcophagi and portrait busts, and in hypogea or along the corridors in catacombs.

For the more affluent, a funerary altar with a portrait or a portrait sculpture provided more opportunities for distinctive commemoration. Veristic portraiture under the Republic, like the famous Barberini Togatus (late first century BCE) who appears to carry two busts of his ancestors, perhaps in a funeral procession (Centrale Montemartini, Rome), depicts the elite with a realism that suggests an individual personality but it also advertises elite status and traditional values with other similarly depicted members.[34] Freedman tombs and portrait reliefs combine non-elite status with the visual vocabulary of the elite, such as women adopting the clothing and gestures of the free born elite, to advertise their freed status and the financial means to purchase land and build a funeral monument for themselves, and often other family members and freedpersons associated with their household.[35] Husbands and wives frequently appear together in portrait reliefs, including on sarcophagi (Chapter II), clasping right hands in evocation of the marriage ceremony. The theme of marriage provided an opportunity to combine the rite of marriage with the rite of funerary commemoration.[36]

The modern continuation of funerary portraiture points to the long legacy of preserving and commemorating the identity of the deceased. Like the ancient Roman dead, modern portraits come in a variety of themes, media, and price points. The monumental tomb of Carolina Gallino (1839–1892) and her family in Staglieno Cemetery, Genoa, sculpted by G. Moreno in 1894, presents the portraits of three generations of family members [**Fig. 13**]. The tomb within a tomb presents a Victorian tableau of a tomb visit in progress. The scene is full of sentimentality and the focus is on the mourners. The daughter of the deceased lifts a child to kiss the portrait bust of her mother. The granddaughter stands on the tips of her toes on top of the tomb to reach her grandmother's face. The daughter looks away as though unable to witness the kiss. The deceased's husband stands facing the spectator with crossed arms, holding his hat, and eyes lowered as though he, too, is unable to bear the sight of the child's kiss. The portraiture of family members (who will themselves be buried in the tomb) is reminiscent of the Barberini Togatus. Both sculpture groups depict many generations of a family within the context of ancestor worship but the understated solemnity of the latter contrasts with the overt sentimentality of the Victorian monument.

Funerary portraits, not in the round, may be in relief, painted, or even photographed. On the Biffani Family monument in Campo Verano

Fig. 13. Gallino Family Funerary Monument. Staglieno Cemetery, Genoa.

Cemetery, Rome [**Fig. 14**], photographs have been added to the reliefs of the original monument. The tomb commemorates the deceased in a design that evokes an ancient funerary altar. It is also reminiscent of the realism of ancient Roman portraiture, in particular freedmen reliefs, by the way that the Biffani family members stare out of their medallions as though looking out of a window. Their clothing is also analogous to Roman funerary portraits – the wife is veiled and her husband wears a toga. The Latin inscription also contextualizes the grave as a Neoclassical revival monument: NON EST IUSTUS MORS ('Death is not just'). A photograph of their son hangs from a medallion between and below the portraits of his parents. The relief sculptures have been replaced by a photograph that is set in contemporary time and provide a further contrast between the portraits of parents and son. The effect of the chronological shift is remarkable since it suggests that the original reliefs are two thousand years older than the contemporary photograph and that the tomb may be a reused ancient monument. The photographs of other family members that are affixed to the

Fig. 14. Biffani Family Funerary Monument. Campo Verano Cemetery, Rome

base of the tomb or on marble plaques that lean against it show that the tomb was active for many generations.

Photographs of the deceased, whether mounted or etched onto the monument itself, are popular on contemporary gravestones, especially photorealistic portraits.[37] The ages of deceased represented in pictures vary and may not be a representation of the age when the person died so a disconnect may result between the age of the deceased in the photograph and the age given on the epitaph. The issue is not so much biological as it is sociological – how one wants to be remembered rather than how one looked the year when one died. A similar dynamic is apparent in some modern obituary notices that give a photograph of the deceased in their youth or even a copy of an official identification photograph such as from their driving licence.

The variety of Roman tomb styles vies for the attention of passers-by to linger and read the inscriptions commemorating the dead. Much like the feature of recent smart phone apps, the cemeteries and tombs offer an 'augmented reality' view of the suburban landscape, and serve as both symbols and texts superimposed against the city, upon arrival, or against the countryside upon departure. 'Reading' the landscape is both a figurative and literal experience. In the case of Statius' *Silvae* 5.3, in which he visits his father's grave, the experience also becomes literally and figuratively timeless. Statius frames his grief in relation to Aeneas' for Anchises in the epic landscape of the *Aeneid*, the 'augmented reality' blends with the legendary and literary past to make the grave at once a real and allusive site.[38]

Tombs are interpretive guides that inform travellers of the identities of former inhabitants commemorated by the tombs, and of current inhabitants doing the commemorating.[39] Epitaphs and portraits on the tombs serve a communicative function beyond identifying the deceased, since many greet passers-by and invite them to read their life's story, thus the dead on the periphery are the first and last, upon entering and exiting the city, to greet travellers, as one-time and recurring representatives of the living within the walls and behind the gates. Seeing the tombs as augmentations, rather than fragmentations of the landscape offers a holistic view of the dead in the suburbs as an extension of the living in the urban centres of cities and towns.

The figurative significance of roadside tombs, however, needs to take into account social elements beyond the representation of the dead, such as the punishment of criminals among tombs that functioned as a highly visible deterrent to potential criminals entering the city and to family members and friends visiting the tombs.[40] After Spartacus' revolt was quelled, for example, 6,000 men were crucified along the Via Appia from Capua to Rome. To punish criminals from the city of Rome, crucifixions were staged outside the Esquiline Gate.[41]

The practicalities involved in making tomb offerings or in travelling along roads produced other associations and strategies: tomb offerings (including live sacrificial animals such as pigs; food, and liquids) and equipment brought from the city on the day of the funeral, on ritually prescribed days following a funeral (Chapter I), or on annual feast days (Chapter IV) and carried some distance, in the case of tombs many miles away from the Aurelianic Walls. On these occasions, the roads would witness multiple scenes of the same activities as travellers pass by others also making the journey or already at tombs taking part in meals. The return trip home would have needed to be made before dark before the closing of the city gates. The problem that distance posed to family members was an opportunity for thieves and robbers who used the isolation of tombs to their advantage. Food offerings left at tombs were subject to theft once the family returned to the city and the tombs provided adequate cover for robbers waiting to ambush passers-by.[42] The remote and death-defined landscape also made it the haunt of ghosts and other supernatural activity.

Gates of the living and the dead

The elite and non-elite in ancient Rome built tombs on privately owned lots. The size and cost of tombs may be an indication of social standing at the time of commemoration but variations between regions make gener-alizations about social status over time difficult to analyse.[43] More impor-tant was the location of tombs. Many aristocrats located tombs close to gates for maximum visible impact to those entering and leaving the city. This prime real estate for the dead mirrored the clustering of elite homes in exclusive areas of the city. The placement of freedmen tombs at city gates signalled a shift in economic/political power as wealth provided the means to vie for exclusive locations. The tomb of M. Vergilius Eurysaces (c. 30 BCE) and possibly other bakers immediately outside Porta Praenestina (Porta Maggiore), for example, practically abuts the gate and the exclusivity and prestige of its location is reinforced by the monumen-tality of its design in the form of an oven with decorative frieze that orig-inally included portrait sculptures of Eurysaces and his wife [**Fig. 15**].[44] For the most part, however, freedmen and other non-elites were buried farther away from the city, but these were interspersed among the elite, whose monumental tombs often signalled the location of an aristocratic estate in the vicinity.[45]

Fig. 15. Tomb of M. Vergilius Eurysaces. Porta Maggiore, Rome.

Family tombs located close to city gates include those of the Fabii (Porta Esquilina), and the Sempronii (located between the Porta Sanqualis and the Porta Salutaris) that survives in the Cortile di San Felice on Via della Dataria across from the Quirinal Palace. The triumphal arch design of this rarely-seen tomb evokes a city gate as though to reference the nearby gates. Other family tombs located close to city gates include the Domitii (Porta Flaminia = Porta del Popolo), the Licinii (between the Porta Salaria and Porta Nomentana), the Claudii Marcelli, the Metelli, and the Servilii (Porta Capena) and the Cornelii (The Tomb of the Scipios) between Porta Capena and Porta Appia (= Porta S. Sebastiano). Elite tombs outside the Porta Capena demonstrate how tombs allowed an opportunity for the promotion and competition of individual and family interests by advertising power through Hellenistic aesthetics and the remodelling of formerly modest tombs on a monumental scale.[46] The same families also built temples and other monuments amidst these tombs that were visible to visitors arriving from the South prior to seeing elite and eponymic

85

monuments in the Forum and Campus Martius.[47] The Porta Capena is no longer extant but the area is still an important entry point into the city and the focus of monumentality. The Ethiopian obelisk from Axum that commemorated Mussolini's Abyssinian victories stood nearby at the UN Food and Agriculture Organization (FAO) before its recent return to Ethiopia. Today, in the Piazza di Porta Capena, two spoliated columns rise in a memorial that evokes the World Trade Center Towers and commemorates the victims of 9/11.

The number of potential sites for tombs in proximity to gates places these more famous family tombs into perspective. North of the city, three major roads led to the gates that bear their names: the Porta Flaminia, Porta Salaria, and Porta Nomentana. The tombs outside Porta Flaminia (Porta del Popolo) and along the Via Flaminia before the first milestone have disappeared but catacombs and a small necropolis are visible at the Basilica of S. Valentino that is roughly halfway between the Porta Flamina and the Milvian Bridge. Beyond the Milvian Bridge the remains of the Tomb of the Nasonii (mid to late second century CE) and three tombs at Casale di Grottarossa (late Republican/early Imperial) are extant.[48]

Outside the Porta Salaria, a necropolis and catacombs were discovered during the construction of the Corso d'Italia that runs along the Aurelianic Wall to the Porta Pinciana.[49] The necropolis is no longer extant but some tombs survive in the vicinity such as the tumulus tomb of M. Lucilius Paetus and his sister Lucilia Polla that is contemporaneous with the Mausoleum of Augustus but was buried under the reign of Trajan with other nearby tombs under a massive layer of soil that later contained tombs of the Hadrianic period on top of the earlier tombs.[50] The diameter of the tomb is about 34 metres and it may have had a conical mound of earth about 17 metres high. A copy of the altar tomb of the boy Q. Sulpicius Maximus is visible in the busy intersection of Piazza Fiume just inside the Aurelianic Wall where it had been incorporated into the Porta Salaria that stood intact until its destruction in 1871 to ease traffic circulation. Farther out on the Via Salaria, the Catacombs of Priscilla preserve Christian burials and the original burial location of many popes between 309 and 555.

The area outside the Porta Nomentana (= Porta Pia) served as a necropolis for the Praetorian camp with tombs along Via Nomentana. Jewish catacombs survive at Villa Torlonia. Travellers arriving to Rome along the Via Nomentana would pass the catacombs and Basilica of S. Alessandro (at the 13 kilometre point). Of all the tombs that were built along this stretch of the road, only the brick core of the Torraccio della Cecchina survives. At the third milestone, the Basilica of S. Agnese fuori le Mura complex, built over a necropolis and the martyr's crypt, contains the remains of the Basilica Constantiniana (built next to the Mausoleum of Constantina/Costanza) that was replaced by the Basilica Honoriana by Pope Honorius I (625–38) after it had fallen into ruin.

From the East, major roads entered the city through the Aurelianic Walls at the Porta Tiburtina and the Porta Praenestina (= Porta Maggiore). Within the wall, the Via Praenestina (following the Via Labicana) led to the Porta Esquilina (= Arch of Gallienus) in the Servian Wall. Outside the Porta Tiburtina, the necropolis that contained the burial crypt of S. Lorenzo became the site of the Basilica of S. Lorenzo fuori le Mura that consists of two basilicas joined end to end in the form of a circus. The Campo Verano Cemetery, located next to the Basilica, preserves the location of the ancient necropolis. The area outside the Porta Esquilina served as a necropolis in the archaic and Republican periods and contained tombs for the elite (such as the Fabii) and for the poor. Funeral professionals resided here in the Grove of Libitina and only entered the city to perform their duties (Chapter I). In the early Imperial period, the area was converted into gardens for Maecenas, thus the dead were buried for a second time and their monuments disappeared from the suburban landscape.[51]

From the Porta Esquilina, the Via Praenestina (following the same course as the Via Labicana) led to Porta Praenestina in the Aurelianic Wall but forked just before reaching it to become Via Praenestina and Via Labicana. The Trajanic cinerary altar of Julia Capriola, now in the Museo Nazionale Romano (Museo delle Terme), was found near the Porta Praenestina. In addition to the monumental Tomb of Eurysaces, built immediately outside the Porta Praenestina, other tombs were found in the area.

The Trajanic funerary stele of the freedwoman Maria Auxesis, on which the deceased reclines on a couch holding a cup, now also in the Museo Nazionale Romano (Museo delle Terme), was found nearby on Via Labicana. The Republican Freedmen tombs on Via Statilia, next to the Aqua Claudia aqueduct, are still visible today incorporated into the wall of a later structure. Along the Via Praenestina away from the city, in the Villa of the Gordiani complex, a basilica in the form of a circus was built next to a monumental round mausoleum, catacombs, and columbaria. At the third milestone of Via Labicana, a Constantinian basilica in the form of a circus was erected at site of the catacombs of Sts. Marcellinus and Peter, near the Imperial mausolea, including St. Helena's tomb (Tor Pignattara).

From the South, the Via Appia left the Porta Capena in the Servian Wall in the direction of two later gates in the Aurelianic Wall, the Porta Latina and the Porta Appia. Outside the Porta Capena, the Tomb of the Scipios contained the sarcophagi of the Cornelii gens, including the sarcophagus of L. Cornelius Scipio Barbatus (consul 298 BCE) and some of the earliest epitaphs that survive.[52] A short distance away is the Columbaria of the Vigna Codini that contained several hypogea tombs from which many urns and marble cippi were discovered. The Columbarium of Pomponius Hylas is situated in the area between Via Latina and Via Appia.[53]

Outside the Porta Latina, important tombs with painted and decorated interiors survive along the Via Latina: the Hypogeum of Trebius Justus (beginning of fourth century CE), the Hypogeum of Via Dino Compagni with tombs decorated with scenes from the Old Testament.[54] Other tombs along the Via Latina are located in the Necropolis of the Fourth Milestone, now a park, which preserves an original section of the Via Latina and numerous tombs, including the so-called Barbarini Tomb, the so-called Tomb of the Valerii, and the Tomb of the Calpurnii. The Basilica of S. Stefano is located close to the Tomb of the Pancratii, whose occupants may be related to the Anicii gens who owned a villa at the location of the current basilica.

Outside the Porta Appia (Porta S. Sebastiano) beyond the Columbarium of Augustus' Freedmen and the Hypogeum of Vibia, many catacomb complexes survive: the Catacombs of S. Callisto, the Catacombs of

Praetextatus and the Jewish Catacombs.[55] The second century CE Tomb of Annia Regilla, wife of Atticus Herodes, also known as the Tempio del Dio Redicolo, on the Via della Caffarella within the Via Appia Archaeological Park area. Opposite the Church of Domine, Quo Vadis? (S. Maria in Palmis), the Tomb of Priscilla is attributed to the wife of Domitian's freedman Abascantus.[56]

The Basilica of S. Sebastiano ad Catacumbas was built in the form of a circus over a necropolis that contained the tomb of S. Sebastiano. The necropolis was active from second to fifth century CE: pagan and Christian burials took place there, and it became the popular source of the word catacomb. Beyond S. Sebastiano, the Catacombs of Domitilla contains Christian burials that were added at the end of the third and beginning of the fourth century CE to earlier pagan burials, such as those of the gens Flavii that date to the end of the second century.[57] Important tombs from this point to beyond the eleventh milestone are still visible among the many concrete cores of tombs no longer extant, including the tomb of Caecilia Metella and tombs restored by Antonio Canova in 1808, such as the tomb of the freedman M. Servilius Quartus and Luigi Canina between 1851 and 1853 and the tomb of the Rabirii (see below).

Western access to the city was through gates in the Aurelianic Wall that bear the names of the major roads that lead to them: the Porta Ostiensis, the Porta Aurelia, and the Porta Cornelia. The Porta Ostiensis (= Porta S. Paolo) stands next to the pyramid tomb of Gaius Cestius that overlooks the Protestant cemetery that, like the adjacent British War Cemetery, preserves the relationship between ancient and modern burial locations but inside the wall rather than outside of it. Outside the Porta S. Paolo, the Basilica S. Paolo fuori le Mura is located next to a necropolis in which tradition places the tomb of St. Paul, but it has not yet been found. Recently, a necropolis was found north of the Basilica that contains five centuries'-worth of burials. Often the strata of tombs are one over the other and illustrate the transition between cremation and inhumation burials between the second and third centuries.[58]

The Porta Aurelia (= Porta S. Pancrazio) on the Janiculum Hill marked the entry point of the Via Aurelia.[59] The remains of S. Pancrazio were located in a nearby necropolis but the basilica built over his tomb by Pope Symmachus (498–515) no longer survives. The later Basilica of S. Pancrazio was built over catacombs that date from the fourth century CE. At the nearby Villa Doria Pamphilj, two columbaria are located behind the Casino del Belrespiro. The larger of the two contained a fresco now in the Museo Nazionale Romano (Museo delle Terme).[60]

The Porta Cornelia (= the later Porta di S. Pietro) in front of the Pons Aelius (=Ponte S. Angelo) allowed access to the city from the West between Porta Aurelia and Porta Flaminia. The Mausoleum of Hadrian was incorporated into the wall at a later date (Honorius). The Aurelianic Wall that followed the Tiber on the left bank does not survive. St. Peter's Necropolis, with pagan and Christian tombs, as well as monuments that survived into the modern era, the Meta Romuli and Terebintus Neronis, were located along Via Cornelia, which follows the modern Via della Conciliazione.[61] The Constantinian Basilica of St. Peter was built against the outer wall of the Circus of Gaius and Nero over St. Peter's tomb and pagan tombs whose roofs and upper levels were removed to serve as the foundation level.

Amidst the burials in St. Peter's Necropolis, a stretch of an ancient road survives, lined with dozens of mausoleum tombs (dating from the second century CE) that were buried when Constantine built his Basilica.[62] The mausolea, in the shape of a 'house', first contained sarcophagi and then inhumation burials in the floor. Remarkable paintings, decoration, mosaics, inscriptions, and sarcophagi survive. The Tomb of the Valerii, one of the largest mausolea in the necropolis, for example, contains Christian paintings and inscriptions that were added at a later date. The Tomb of the Caetennii (second century CE) preserves its interior decoration of architectural details, while the Tomb of the Julii (Severan in date) contains Christian paintings of Jonah and the Good Shepherd, but also a mosaic in the vault of Christ depicted as the sun god Helios in his chariot. In addition to these mausolea, relatively few of these so-called house tombs survive in Rome: only the remains of a house tomb on the Via Appia that is Augustan in date and three pagan tombs in the necropolis of S. Sebastiano in Catacumbas.

More examples are extant in the contemporary Isola Sacra/Portus Necropolis, Ostia Antica, many of which preserve dining couches at the entrance for ritual meals (see Chapter IV for illustration and discussion). The Isola Sacra/Portus Necropolis and the Via Laurentina Necropolis preserve the second/third century CE roadside tombs with collective burials of the middle-class/lower-class burials. Tombs could face the road or be located in rows behind the street-facing row. The so-called house tombs were built for collective cremation burials with niches to store containers and arcosolia (semi-circular niches in the wall that could accommodate a sarcophagus), and preserve evidence for the increase in inhumation burials at the time of the Emperor Hadrian with burials in the floor and in *arcosolia* formerly used for cremation inhumation. The term 'house tombs' used to describe these tombs is misleading since they evoke house façades (to us) rather than replicate actual ancient Roman house design, in which building took place around a central atrium.[63] Some tombs had benches in front of the entrance door for ritual meals (Chapter IV), traces of which are visible in front of the row of 'house tombs' 77–81 [**Fig. 16**]. More modest burials

Fig. 16. Tombs 77–81. Isola Sacra/Portus Necropolis.

at Isola Sacra include two roof tiles leaned against each other to form a roof over a mound; cement vaults, or lean-to burials added against the outer walls of tombs, which encroached upon the monuments of others.

Mausolea in the form of so-called house tombs have an enduring history in Western burial practices. Unlike their Roman precursors, modern house tombs evoke actual homes, and thus encourage the metaphor of a home for deceased family members. Père-Lachaise Cemetery, Paris, and New Orleans cemeteries are particularly famous for burial vaults in the shape of houses. At Lafayette Cemetery No. 1, for example, the tombs line roads and alleys and are evocative of ancient tombs [**Fig. 17**]. Due to the ground water level, burials must be above ground. As a Catholic burial ground, all of the burials were inhumation until the recent lifting of the cremation ban. The house tombs are too small to allow for entry; rather, the deceased are placed in a chamber, open to the outside, that is then faced with brick and plaster. The body is stored on top until decomposition and then removed and stored in the pit below the tomb (*caveau*) by the so-called 'bag and tag' method, as described by a guide during a tour of the cemetery. This allows for multiple burials above or when ownership of the tomb changes. The oldest cemetery in New Orleans, St. Louis Cemetery No. 1, was under a foot and a half of water following Hurricane Katrina, so the homes of both the living and the dead were flooded.

Legacy of Roman tombs

Due to the centuries-long neglect and destruction of tombs along the roads leading to/from Rome, it is not possible to gauge the effect of walking within a necropolis on a tomb-lined road outside of an ancient city. The Via Appia Antica comes closest to giving an impression of the experience but outside of Rome, extant tombs survive at archaeological sites in greater number and in their original locations. At the archaeological site of ancient Pompeii, for example, numerous tombs and cenotaphs are still in situ outside the Nucerian and Herculaneum Gates, and give a sense of the periphery of

Fig. 17. Lafayette Cemetery No. 1. New Orleans, LA.

the dead but on a smaller scale than the miles of tombs that once lined the major roads in ancient Rome.[64]

Following the collapse of Rome, tombs and cemeteries would give pilgrims their first impression of the city and serve as metaphors for the defunct city that lay in ruins inside the gates. In the twelfth century CE *Mirabilia Urbis Romae* of Canon Benedict, 22 cemeteries and catacombs are listed among attractions of interest to pilgrims, many of which were still visible outside the city gates, including those outside the Porta Salaria, Porta Appia, Porta Latina, Porta Tiburtina, and the Porta Ostiensis. Two modern cemeteries survive in the locations of these ancient cemeteries close to the Aurelianic Walls: the Campo Verano Cemetery which Canon Benedict lists as the Cemetery of the *Ager Veranus* at San Lorenzo fuori le Mura and the modern Protestant Cemetery, inside and outside the Porta Ostiense, which is now located inside the Aurelianic Wall. Just how much the periphery of the dead formed an integral part of the topography of Rome along its perimeter well beyond antiquity and the time of Canon Benedict is apparent by the numerous cemeteries and roadside tombs that were located near to city gates outside both the Servian and Aurelianic walls.

The legacy of the dead on the periphery is one of Christian continuation and redefinition of pagan sites. Christian burials were added to earlier pagan burials so the sites of martyr and saint burials were located in close proximity to pagan ones and venerated among them, as at St. Peter's Necropolis and the necropolis and catacombs at S. Sebastiano ad Catacumbas. Some cemeteries along the Aurelianic Wall, along with others farther out along the roads leading to Rome, became the site of basilicas under Constantine and early Popes, which were built over martyr tombs and named after the saint whose burial redefined the pagan necropolis. This redefinition of both cemetery and periphery now denoted persons and the sites of their martyrdom as important figures and events in early Christian history and gave later Christians in the fourth century CE and beyond a narrative that depended upon, but was defined by, the reigns of pagan emperors.

Basilicas also served as architectural transitions when catacombs were abandoned in the fourth century CE for open-air burials, in that they preserved martyr tombs and catacombs below but they also served as a backdrop and focal point to contemporary above-ground burials. The consular roads, lined with tombs that formerly led to the city gates, now lead to the basilicas built on Imperial lands located close to the Aurelianic Walls as a physical and figurative Christian pomerium. Christian sites and symbols functioned as a form of augmented reality to define the landscape and the journey to/from Rome. This teleological redefinition of both the pagan city and its periphery redefined the suburban and urban landscape prior to the construction of basilicas closer to the centre of the city. Although many of the saints and martyr remains and relics were later translated to churches inside the walls, the catacombs with the burials of unknown Christians continued to serve as sites of veneration and pilgrimage, from the time of Canon Benedict to the present.

It seems remarkable that of the large number of burials in ancient Rome, in particular those lining the roads, relatively few monuments survive. The large number of *tituli* that survive or were recorded prior to their destruction suggest that thousands of tombs once made up the periphery of the dead. Since erosion due to environmental changes caused by industrial and vehicular pollution is a relatively recent phenomenon, the destruction of the tombs was deliberate.[65] The House of Lorenzo Manilio in the Ghetto of Rome (begun in 1468) is a famous example of the reuse of various funerary monument fragments as building material. An inscription on the facade makes Manilio's Classical referencing to ancient Rome explicit. The building is now home to many businesses, including a café-bar, over the entrance of which the portraits of three family members from a freedman relief stare back at those entering, or seem like apartment owners looking out of their window at passers-by.

Tombs had already been used as building material during the construction of Aurelianic Wall and later reconstructions and repairs of the wall, gates, and towers. The Pyramid of Cestius is the most famous tomb that was incorporated into the Aurelianic Wall, but the incorporation of tombs into the Wall was common at the time of its construction and during the later reconstruction of gates and towers, especially during the reign of Honorius. Other tombs incorporated into the Wall include the tomb of Q. Sulpicius Maximus into the Porta Salaria; the tomb of L. Ofilius that was incorporated into a tower of Porta Tiburtina; the tomb of Eurysaces at Porta Praenestina (= Porta Maggiore) that was incorporated into a tower; an early Imperial tomb near Porta San Sebastiano beyond the eleventh tower just past Bastion of Sangallo; and a Severan tomb with painted lunettes, including one of Prometheus, that was incorporated into the portcullis chamber between the two towers of Porta Ostiense. Additions to the fortifications of the gates continued into the modern era. Sixtus IV (1471–1484), for example, built square towers (no longer extant) on either side of Porta del Popolo by using large marble blocks taken from several nearby tombs.[66]

Roadside tombs had been used every 25 years from 1300 to 1800 for the repair of roads that served as pilgrim routes. The destruction was reversed by Pope Pius IX, who restored the Via Appia Antica in the seventh year of his long pontificate (1846–1878). Pius IX entrusted oversight of the restoration to the archaeologist and architect Luigi Canina from 1851–1853. A medal that Pope Pius IX issued to commemorate the restoration suggests more tombs than actually survive or were reconstructed: on the reverse side, monuments along the Via Appia Antica are displayed like a tourist ad under the Latin motto: VIA APPIA RESTITUTA ('Via Appia Restored'). Rows of tombs are shown on either side disappearing into the horizon. In the foreground is the statue of the dying St. Sebastian that is displayed directly above his tomb in the Basilica of S. Sebastiano ad Catacumbas. The basilica is prominently displayed on the right side of the coin with the tomb of Caecilia Metella on the left.[67] The restoration connects the Basilica of S. Sebastiano ad Catacumbas, one of the seven pilgrim churches until the Jubilee in 2000, and Christian burials in the catacombs (S. Sebastiano, S. Callisto, etc) along the Via Appia Antica to the Church of Domine, Quo Vadis? (S. Maria in Palmis) located just outside of the Porta S. Sebastiano, that was built at the site where tradition claims that St. Peter, upon his arrival in Rome, encountered Christ. Thus, Pius IX restored a Roman consular road once lined with pagan burials, temples, and monuments into a Christian route for pilgrims who retrace Peter's steps into Rome through the periphery of Christian burials.[68] The site remains an archaeological park today and preserves the rustic appearance of Rome before its growth into a modern metropolitan city.

In addition to a route taken by pilgrims, the Via Appia Antica was also a destination that was visited on the Grand Tour. Giovanni Battista Piranesi's etching 'Via Appia Imaginaria' (1756), shows a fantasy recreation of lavish tombs and monuments but the tombs had all but disappeared except for a few monumental structures, such as the tomb of Caecilia Metella that had been converted into a fortress, or those whose concrete and brick interiors, already stripped of marble facing and sculptural reliefs, remained as reminders of their former function. Nevertheless, in other prints, Piranesi and other artists used the surviving monuments and tombs to contrast the Classical grandeur of Rome with its contemporary appearance of ancient ruins among medieval and baroque architecture and countryside that still contained vineyards, olive groves, and orchards.

The Via Appia Antica exemplified this pastoral setting and was visited by Northern European, British, and North American travellers on the

Fig. 18. John Linton Chapman, 'Via Appia' 1867. Georgia Museum of Art,
University of Georgia.

Grand Tour who contemplated Rome's grandeur and famous figures before
indifferent Roman peasants grazing their herds. Grand Tour travellers in
the nineteenth century continued to visit the Via Appia Antica that had
changed little since Piranesi's time. American John Linton Chapman's
painting, 'Via Appia' (1867), now in the Georgia Museum of Art, shows
a pastoral scene amidst the remains of tombs with a view of St. Peter's in
the distance [**Fig. 18**].[69] In the foreground, goatherds rest on the Tomb
of the Rabirii and behind them the ruins of the aqueducts along the horizon.
The funerary monuments of the Classical past introduce and serve as the
teleological focus of Papal Rome, which literally and figuratively arises in
the distance from its ruins. The image, however, is fantasy like Pianesi's
'Via Appia Imaginaria'.

Chapman manipulated the locations of the tombs to achieve his perspec-
tive of St. Peter's dome. On the right side the Tomb of the Rabirii, restored
by Luigi Canina, is in the foreground next to a brick tomb (known as Laterizio
I because of the *opus latericium* brickwork and also restored by Canina).
The brick tomb is in the correct location on the right hand side of the Via
Appia but the Tomb of the Rabirii is actually 500m away on the other side
of the Via Appia to the right as you leave Rome. To achieve his perspective,
Chapman first painted the brick tomb looking towards Rome but then set
up his easel facing the opposite direction to add the Tomb of the Rabirii in
the foreground on the right in the place where a brick tomb known as

Fig. 19. Tomb of the Rabirii. Via Appia Antica, Rome.

Laterizio II is actually situated, next to Laterizio I looking towards Rome. The Tomb of the Rabirii survives along a tree-lined Via Appia [**Fig. 19**], but a plaster cast of the relief has replaced the original, which is now in the Museo Nazionale Romano (Palazzo Massimo alle Terme).

Neoclassicism

The Pyramid tomb of Gaius Cestius and its relation and proximity to the Protestant Cemetery, Rome, played an important role in the spread of Neoclassicism in funerary architecture, which also includes stele, altars, temples, columns, obelisks, sculpture, sarcophagi, and urns as design elements [**Fig. 11**]. The Pyramid evokes the Hellenistic pyramids of Ptolemaic Egypt (which had themselves been inspired by the Pharaonic pyramids). The tomb, made of brick that is faced with marble, was constructed after 18 BCE and measures 27m high. The tomb is part of the Egyptianising movement begun by Augustus, who transformed the topography of Rome following his defeat of Mark Antony and Cleopatra at the Battle of Actium, 31 BCE. Evocations of Alexandria and Egypt took on political and military significance through Augustus' introduction of obelisks to Rome for the central spine of the Circus Maximus and for his Mausoleum complex, which included a sundial (Horologium) and the Ara Pacis. Today, the pyramid serves as a backdrop to the Neoclassical monuments in the Protestant Cemetery but it also derives meaning as the marker of nearby graves, especially those of Shelley and Keats. Charles Dickens, *Pictures from Italy* (1844): "From one part of the city, looking out beyond the walls, a squat and stunted pyramid (the burial-place of Caius Cestius) makes an opaque triangle in the moonlight. But, to an English traveller, it serves to mark the grave of Shelley too, whose ashes lie beneath a little garden near it. Nearer still, almost within its shadow, lie the bones of Keats, 'whose name is writ in water,' that shines brightly in the landscape of a calm Italian night." Thomas Hardy, in his poem "Rome at the Pyramid of Cestius near the Graves of Shelley and Keats (1901)," also makes the connection explicit to the disadvantage of Cestius whose life and death are rated as secondary to those of Shelley and Keats:

> [...] This I know: in death all silently
> He does a finer thing,
>
> In beckoning pilgrim feet
> With marble finger high
> To where, by shadowy wall and history-haunted street,
> Those matchless singers lie...
>
> – Say, then, he lived and died
> That stones which bear his name
> Should mark, through Time, where two immortal Shades abide;
>
> It is an ample fame.

It is an irony of urban planning that the Pyramid of Cestius inspired Neoclassical design but that two other pyramid tombs in Rome that had survived antiquity were removed because of their associations with non-Christian burials in pagan Rome. Pope Alexander VI (1492–1503) removed

Fig. 20. Funerary Monument of Cardinal Leopoldo Calcagnini by Pietro Bracci. S. Andrea delle Fratte, Rome.

the pyramid tomb known as the *Meta di Borgo* or the *Meta Romuli* in the Middle Ages (since it formed a pair with the Pyramid of Cestius that was known as the *Meta Remi*) to widen the Via Alexandrina (Via della Conciliazione) and to remove a pagan symbol so close to St. Peter's Square.[70] The tomb appears in the fresco 'The Vision of the Cross' painted by the Circle of Raphael (1520–1524), including Giulio Romano, in the Sala di Constantino, part of the Raphael Rooms in the Vatican Museums.

That another pyramid of unknown name was removed to build S. Maria dei Miracoli in seventeenth century is ironic, since it would have fit the Neoclassical reworking of the Piazza by Domenico Fontana that was later realized by Giuseppe Valadier in 1823. As part of Pope Sixtus V's urban plan, Fontana moved the obelisk from the Circus Maximus (where the emperor Augustus had erected it following its removal from Heliopolis after his victory over Antony and Cleopatra) and erected it in the Piazza in 1589. The pyramid would have fit the design scheme but its replacement by a church follows the pattern of the removal of the Tomb of the Domitii to build S. Maria del Popolo on the other side of the Piazza del Popolo.

The pyramid is an important design element of Neoclassical funerary monuments. Raphael designed the Chigi Chapel (1513–16) for the banker Agostino Chigi as an octagonal temple that included two pyramid tombs (and designs for a third pyramid that would have been visible below the floor). The chapel was incomplete at the time of Raphael's death in 1520 but the tombs were completed to his design by Lorenzetto and later reworked by Gian Lorenzo Bernini in 1652. Bernini's addition of the portrait medallions of Agostino Chigi and his brother Sigismondo Chigi and later the addition of angels and

Fig. 21. Funerary Monument of Giovanni Volpato by Antonio Canova. Ss. Apostoli, Rome.

allegories to the pyramid composition, such as his funerary monument for the De Silva family in Sant' Isidoro, Rome (1663), contributed to Raphael's Neoclassic vocabulary and had a profound influence on funerary monuments.[71]

The tomb of Cardinal Leopoldo Calcagnini (1746–9), designed by Pietro Bracci (known mostly for his statues of Oceanus/Neptune and the Tritons with horses in the Trevi Fountain (1759–62) and the tombs of Pope Benedict XIII and Pope Benedict XIV in St. Peter's Basilica), is located in S. Andrea delle Fratte.[72] Bracci combines the pyramid with a portrait of Cardinal Calcagnini painted in an oval medallion [**Fig. 20**]. An eagle and garland sit atop the medallion and the pyramid appears supported by a lion looking up towards an angel, who is in the act of writing an epitaph on the pyramid. The self-referentiality of the monument is unique among tombs of this type, and gives the spectator the impression that the tomb and epitaph will be completed momentarily. Bracci's output of funerary monuments was impressive and among his famous commissions centred on the pyramid are the Tomb of Maria Clementina Sobieski in St. Peter's Basilica and the Tomb of Cardinal Fabrizio Paolucci in S. Marcello al Corso.

Like Bernini and his Baroque imitators, Antonio Canova expanded the Neoclassical vocabulary of funerary monuments. Canova makes the connection between the deceased and antiquity explicit in his monument for the engraver Giovanni Volpato (1807) at the Basilica of Ss. Apostoli [**Fig. 21**]. The monument shows a bust of Volpato atop a stele with an allegorical female figure that is seated opposite and grieves with lowered head. A garland is wrapped around Volpato's portrait, which sits on top of a column inscribed with an epitaph. There is a timeless quality to the memorial that is evocative of ancient Greek steles.[73] The realism of Volpato's portraiture, however, is closer to freedmen reliefs, contrasts with the generic quality of Greek funerary reliefs, and introduces an ephemeral element that alludes to the brevity of life. Canova restored many tombs along the Via Appia around this date (such as the tomb of M. Servilius Quartus that was restored to his design in 1808) and his knowledge of ancient tombs informs his own designs, often with unexpected and innovative results.

The monumental tomb that Canova designed for Archduchess Maria

Fig. 22. Funerary Monument of Erasmo di Giuseppe Piaggio.
Staglieno Cemetery, Genoa.

Christina of Austria (1798–1805) in the Augustiner Kirche, Vienna, is the culmination of Neoclassic pyramid tomb design, which elaborates on the iconography and scale (5.74m) of the designs of Raphael, Bernini, and Bracci. The tomb is in the shape of a pyramid that has an entrance evoking the Pyramid of Cestius more than the pyramids in relief of Canova's precursors. A portrait of the Archduchess appears in a medallion held up by a flying allegorical figure that is accompanied by a young angel. The portrait forms the literal and figurative apex of the tomb. Below the medallion and centred above the entrance is a Latin inscription dedicated by her husband Prince Albert, Archduke of Saxony-Teschen: UXORI · OPTIMAE/ALBERTUS ('Albert to his Excellent Wife'). The Archduchess' name does not appear on the monument. A procession of allegorical figures that represent various stages of life carry an urn containing the remains, and a garland that connects the figures makes its way into the monument. The figures walk upon a rug that connects the interior of the tomb to the outside world of the mourners. To the right of the entrance, are the figures of an angel and lion grieving against a heraldic shield. The highly allusive tomb commemorates and frames both the deceased and the grief of her husband in relation to Classical antiquity and earlier Neoclassical monuments in an Imperial setting.

The pyramid tomb design endured as a design motif to the Neoclassical Revival in late nineteenth century. The funerary monumental of Erasmo di Giuseppe Piaggio (1799–1874) in Staglieno Cemetery, Genoa, features a bearded angel who sits atop a sarcophagus tub with arms and legs folded [**Fig. 22**]. His foot hangs out from the statue base at almost the eye level of the viewer. Behind the angel is a pyramid with a portrait of the deceased but without a medallion frame. On top of the pyramid is a bronze cross and anchor set in a spray of roses. The facial expression of the angel is as remarkable as his pose. Unlike his Baroque precursors, he is not assisting in the death of the deceased or writing his epitaph on the pyramid. Rather, he seems as though he is pausing in a conversation momentarily lost in thought more than he is grieving or brooding over the death of the deceased, atop whose tomb he sits ready to resume his conversation with a passer-by. This monument attests to the popularity of Neoclassical tomb designs centred on pyramids over three centuries after Raphael's design of the Chigi Chapel.

Classical imitations and evocations extend the significance of ancient monuments to contemporary imitators as they extend the periphery of the dead to countries and continents beyond ancient borders. Chronology and geography are less important, however, than the (self-) identifications of the dead who are commemorated and their imitative commemorators. Chapter IV explores further how the literal and figurative boundaries between the living and the dead are negotiated through ongoing social interactions which perpetuate the identities of the dead through repeated ritual observances on special holidays. Like the ancients who shared food and drink with the dead, modern practices provide opportunities for communion with the dead with rituals that are at once, solemn and celebratory.

CHAPTER IV

CULT OF THE DEAD

The 91 year-old widow lived by herself in a tumbledown house on a desolate country road. But she wasn't alone, not really, not as long as she could visit her husband and twin sister. No matter they were already dead. Jean Stevens simply had their embalmed corpses dug up and stored them at her house – in the case of her late husband, for more than a decade – tending the remains as best she could until police were finally tipped off last month. [...] 'I think when you put them in the (ground), that's goodbye, goodbye,' Stevens said. 'In this way I could touch her and look at her and talk to her'.[1]

The normally figurative reintegration of and socialising with the dead becomes an extreme literal one in Stevens' case, of continued social interactions with the corpses of her husband and twin sister. The digging up of the corpses represents a reversal of burial and a denial of their death to one who was not fully ready to accept life without them. Her description of burial as 'goodbye, goodbye' suggests that Stevens' partially accepted the deaths of her husband and sister but that she was not able to part with them physically and so lived with them in her home as though they were still alive.

The need to keep the dead physically close is a sign of Stevens' grief and loneliness, similar to the figurative retention of the dead in the home that was the site of former social interactions. In the case of artwork and portraits made from the cremated remains of family members that hang in the house (Chapter II), however, the retention is both literal and figurative. The dead may be buried and commemorated elsewhere but the continued association of domestic space with the dead signals a need to retain a physical connection with them – an acceptance of the biology of a person's death where they are now disposed but an inability to accept the emotional and social reality of their death at the place where they once lived.

In the *New York Times Magazine* feature, 'The Shrine Down the Hall', photographer Ashley Gilbertson photographed the bedrooms of the war dead that had not changed since the day they left for combat duty.[2] Like Roman atria that contained the shrines and portraits of ancestors (Chapter II), the bedrooms are shrines to the dead where the living continue to be in 'their space' as though they could walk through the front door at any moment and return to their bedrooms, which look the same as the day they left them. The photographs document both the lives lost and the lives of survivors who continue to feel the impact of their deaths. The bedroom shrines allow for continued socialisation with the dead, who are figuratively frozen in time: they are the age that they attained at the time of their death and they are the age symbolised by the bedroom décor as they left it prior combat duty. A shrine in the home allows survivors the privacy and the time needed to mourn the death of a loved one.

The home is one of many possible sites with which to associate the dead with their former lives and to commemorate their death (besides place of disposal). Roadside memorials along highways, whether flowers, crosses, balloons, stuffed animals, or written messages, provide an opportunity to mark the place where someone died but also the place where they were last alive.[3] The memorials that are visible to motorists also serve as cautionary symbols especially at dangerous curves and other high-risk road points, and are part of the landscape that keep the memory of the accident victim alive and provide evidence for their commemoration by the living, who maintain the shrines. Pavement memorials that mark the place where someone was killed have a similar effect on the urban landscape. The memorials provide evidence for the commemoration of the deceased in a setting that juxtaposes the moment of death with the ongoing commemoration of the victim's life in a lived environment in which passers-by may know nothing of the memorial's significance, amidst the activity and visual markers of urban life.

Memorials perpetuate an identity for the deceased and provide focal points for ongoing social relationships, but reminiscences and conversations with the dead are not confined to a particular location or triggered only by a visit to a memorial. As with commemoration, the internet is changing how we literally and figuratively communicate with the dead to further break down the periphery of death and to remove barriers that confine commemoration to a particular location, event, or commemorative holiday. Messages from the dead are traditionally sought through voodoo, séances, or even Electronic Voice Phenomenon (EVP) recordings popularised by television ghost hunters, but conversations and messages that are saved on answering machines and voicemail preserve the actual voice of the deceased in previously recorded messages. The loss or accidental erasing of these messages may cause the recipient to experience the death of a loved one anew. The case of an 80-year-old widower whose saved voicemail message of his wife was deleted by a phone service upgrade captured media attention, and eventually led to its restoration after the telephone company had said that deletions were permanent.[4]

The internet, however, allows for final conversations to take place through websites such as mylastemail.com, which allows someone to compose email messages to friends and foes alike to be delivered after the death of the sender has been confirmed. Unexpected and comforting final words from a loved one may provide solace but the shock of receiving a message from an enemy may be followed by frustration that a return email cannot be sent nor read by the vengeful sender. The dead may maintain a presence on social network sites. Before a profile is sealed or 'memorialised', friends may still visit the deceased's page and see their final postings or receive an invitation to reconnect with them. Even after a profile is sealed or 'memorialized' on Facebook and the digital death of the user is acknowledged, messages can still be left on their wall. In addition, Facebook groups allow for memorial

Fig. 23. Grave marker of Nino Cordio. Protestant Cemetery, Rome.

pages that provide a means for family and friends to maintain a social connection with the deceased and with each other.

This chapter focuses on the dead as undead; in particular, the ongoing social relationships between the living and the dead in which the living continue to perpetuate an identity for the deceased through memorials, epitaphs, and graveside rituals. The Neoclassical and Victorian monuments that derived meaning from Classical antiquity have given way to contemporary means of commemoration, such as virtual online memorials and cemeteries, automobile decals, and tattoos, which communicate the identities of the dead as modern memorials and epitaphs. Commemoration is becoming a literal and figurative moving experience, actual or digital, that no longer requires funerary monuments or visits to cemeteries for continued interactions and conversations with the dead who retain their identity and social significance. Visiting the graves of the famous, and the display and viewing of the dead in museum exhibitions, further removes the periphery of death and further integrates the dead into the urban fabric of modern culture.

(Self-) Identifying the dead

When Pliny (*Letters* 6.10) visited the tomb of the general Verginius Rufus (who had suppressed the revolt of Vindex in 68 CE), he was dismayed to find that the monument was still unfinished nine years after his death due to the neglect of the person responsible for its construction. The place where his remains are located is known but without proper commemoration of the deceased to give both the tomb and Verginius Rufus' life accomplishments meaning. To Pliny, the burial site and therefore commemoration is incomplete for one deserving of both. This neglect of the tomb and suitable memorialisation is a source of anxiety for those fearing similar mistreatment: 'For who is not afraid of what we see happened to Verginius? The wrong of which, his fame makes even more conspicuous since it is undeserved?'[5]

In contrast with leaving one's commemoration to others, the Sicilian artist Nino Cordio designed his own grave marker in the Protestant Cemetery, Rome, to commemorate his life and art [**Fig. 23**], and was thus in control of his own identification even in death.[6] The grave marker itself is a work of art that bears the artist's own signature.[7] It appears against a blank tombstone where one expects the epitaph, as though Cordio has signed a work of art; but since the canvas, as it were, is blank, the signature declares his life was his art and his art was his life. The epitaph (PITTORE INCISORE SCULTORE/ SANTA NINFA 10·7·1937/ ROMA 24·4·2000) and a small bronze pomegranate appear on a long slab that evokes ancient mausolea benches upon which corpses were left to corrupt. The artist's body, however, is replaced and signified by the pomegranate, itself a symbol of death that was an important and frequent subject of Cordio's sculpture so its inclusion on the monument also alludes to his artistic oeuvre, including the monumental Pomegranate Fountain in the Piazza di Santa Ninfa.

Due to the high costs of burials today, monumental graves of a few generations ago are no longer prevalent. For contemporary grave markers, granite has largely replaced marble and sandstone since it is more durable. The typical size of a headstone that often records one or several names, plus biographical information, provides less opportunity for individualisation beyond the selection of the colour of stone, the font of the epitaph inscription and the inclusion of images, whether portraits or symbols, such as flowers or the emblems of a lodge or fraternal order. Modern grave markers for Christian burials which include biblical quotations or symbols of salvation are common, such as a bible, cross, sun, or roses, which reflect continuity with early Christian burials, decorated with symbols such as fish and good shepherd. A menorah is common on Jewish tombs. The use of a funeral marker as identifier, however, is not universal since there are no tombstones for Sikhs.

Engraved memorial monuments are being supplemented by a recorded message that gives a narrative of the deceased's identity and life accomplishments. The 'Personal Rosetta Stone' provides mp3 recordings that can be motion-detected or manually accessed from a tombstone. The stone literally speaks to a visitor or passer-by, like an artefact in an interactive museum exhibition, and gives an innovative way for the self-representation of the dead in a cemetery beyond a burial monument or marker.[8] In addition to addressing visitors, tombs may also be used to advocate an issue that was important to the deceased. The line 'Smoking killed me' relates a health message at the place of burial and provides a posthumous statement from the deceased to contextualize the date of their death.[9]

The information contained on Greek and Latin epitaphs varies from names, generic messages to wayfarers to contemplate the tomb and the shortness of life or to leave flowers, biographical details, the listing of virtues, specifications for sacrifices and other graveside rituals, and formulae that express wishes for a peaceful rest (*sit tibi terra levis; somno aeterno*). In ancient Rome, the measurements of the tomb and plot of land, and even legally enforceable prohibitions against adding unauthorised burials or abusing the tomb were common.

There is comparatively less evidence for and less information on Greek epitaphs than Roman ones. It is difficult, therefore, to talk about identification or self-identification among Greeks due to stylized idealised monuments and often, only the name of the deceased and their attainment of virtuous ideals, such as bravery or modesty (*sophrosyne*), but rarely piety to dead ancestors (unlike Romans).[10] The epitaphs, like the tombs, seem to occupy a timeless present as the following select examples illustrate even with biographical information. The stele of Ampharete (c. 430–420 BCE) in the Kerameikos Museum, for example, depicts a veiled woman who is seated holding a baby on her lap that appears to be a mother and child but the inscription identifies as her as a grandmother holding her grandchild: 'I hold my daughter's son, whom I used to hold on my knees when we both looked upon the light of the sun: now, I, dead, hold him, also dead'.[11] The stele may have been pre-made and the epitaph adapted to personalize the monument for Ampharete but one cannot rule out the possibility that it was designed with her in mind.

More biographical information appears on the epitaph of a certain Socratea from Paros:

> Nicandros was my father, my homeland Paros, and my name was
>   Socratea. When I died, my husband Parmenion buried me
> in this grave to grant me the favour of a memorial of my
>   well-esteemed life even for those to come.
> The Erinyes of child-bearing whom none can guard against
>   destroyed my sweet life through a haemorrhage.
> Nor by my travail did I bring the child into the light
>   but he lies here among the dead in my womb.[12]

Socratea's epitaph gives the cause of her own and her child's death. The first person narrative of her death in childbirth makes the inscription more poignant. The emphasis on her father and husband is a reminder of women's identification through their relationship with men in a male-centred social hierarchy and the death of the child reinforces the dangers women faced to produce an heir to perpetuate a family's lineage. The epitaph also presents the reader with the image of a burial within a burial: the child is still in the womb and both mother and child are buried in the earth.

Epitaphs that emphasise the virtue of the deceased may be very brief and give only a glimpse of the personality of the person commemorated: 'In her embrace, Callisto, earth has hidden your body,/but to your friends you have left the memory of your virtue'.[13] The nurturing role of Mother Earth in embracing Callisto in death seems deserved and the perpetuation of her memory through the recollection of her virtue produces the remarkable effect of distinguishing the dead body of Callisto with the live memory of her character that outlives her.

The formula of wishing a peaceful rest under a light cover of earth appears on both pagan and Christian epitaphs. In an epitaph from Rhodes in the third century BCE, a contrast is made between the body that is buried and the soul that is now in Hades: 'Fare well even in Hades, and lightly may earth cover you.'[14] In a Christian epitaph from Athens that dates around the fourth or fifth century CE, the contrast between the physical remains

Fig. 24. Plaque from the Tomb of Scribonia Attice.
Isola Sacra/Portus Necropolis.

of the deceased and their soul remains but rather than Hades, it resides in Heaven among Christian souls as it did prior to birth: 'Earth covers the body here, but the soul has flown/ into the air, and is among those as it was before./For it has received this reward for honest character.'[15]

Information on the social relationships of the buried dead is possible based on the proximity of burials of family members, such as the Koroibos family (above) or Kimon Koalemos, who won the four-horse chariot race three times in a row at Olympia and was allegedly killed by Pisistratus' sons in 527 BCE. He was given a prominent burial location outside of Athens that was exploited by other family members.[16] These are among the few exceptions, however, since it is difficult to reconstruct the original locations of tomb monuments in museums whose exact locations were not documented or known at the time of their discovery.

Latin epitaphs contain more biographical information about the deceased and their relationship with family members.[17] The inclusion of portraits and plaques add further opportunities for the identification and self-identification of the dead to control the message communicated by funerary monument. The tomb of the surgeon M. Ulpius Amerimnus and his wife Scribonia Attice, a midwife, in the Isola Sacra/ Portus Necropolis (Tomb 100), for example, contains two plaques on either side of the entrance and epitaphs that commemorate their occupations. The surgeon is depicted seated in front of a patient whose leg is being bled. Surgeon implements are displayed next to the procedure in progress. The plaque of his wife shows her performing the duties of a midwife. She sits on a stool with her arm extended between the legs of a woman about to give birth. The mother-to-be is seated with her hands gripping handles as a woman standing behind her assists in the delivery [**Fig. 24**]. The plaques are not portraits but rather commemorations and in-progress representations of the lives led (and saved) by the deceased at the location of their burial.

The identification of a tomb, marker, sarcophagus, urn, or catacomb niche may be very brief and include only the name of the deceased, but communication between the deceased and a passer-by on an epitaph on a roadside memorial may contain a combination of biographical information, expression of a *memento mori* message, formulae for the peaceful rest of the deceased, prohibition against abusing the grave or infringing on its borders, and the dimensions of the burial plot. The terse epitaph of Pontia Prima identifies the grave and prohibits its abuse: 'Pontia Prima/ here lies buried./ Do not damage.'[18] The epitaph of Marcus Statius Chilo combines several themes:

Here lies Marcus Statius Chilo, freedman of Marcus
Alas, weary traveller, you who are passing by me,
Even though you may journey for a long time,
Nevertheless, you will come to this same place.
Frontage 10 feet, depth 10 feet.[19]

The formula of wishing for the earth to lie light (*sit tibi terra levis*) represents a communication to the dead on a memorial on which the identity of the dead is communicated to the living. The epitaph of Optatus expresses the grief of his parents and also recalls the transformation of Flavia Nicopolis' ashes into flowers (see above):

Here lies Optatus, an infant well known for his affection,
    whose ashes, I pray, may be violets and roses,
and the earth, who is now his mother, I pray will be light on him,
    for the boy's life was a burden to none.
Therefore, all that his wretched parents can do,
    they have set up this epitaph for their son.[20]

The formula may also be reversed and extended from the deceased to the reader of his/her epitaph: 'This monument was made for Marcus Caecilius./ Stranger, thank you for stopping at my resting place./ Good luck, good health, and may you sleep without care.'[21] The conversational tone and the well wishes are indicative of the social nature of Latin epitaphs that make the viewing/reading of them part of an on-going relationship with the dead.

Pagan epitaphs are often addressed to the *Manes* of the dead: *Dis Manibus* 'to the spirits of the dead', often abbreviated to *D.M.*, followed by the name of the deceased and/or other biographical information or formulae depending on the size and cost of the monument or marker, sarcophogus, urn, or *titulus* plaque.[22] The gods of the Underworld are also invoked to protect the burial site: 'I ask by the Stygian gods, whoever you are, that you do not disturb our bones nor violate this place of burial.'[23] In some Christian epitaphs, *D.M.* is retained but appears with Christian symbols or the monogram of Christ: 'May your *Manes* be blessed by our prayers.'[24] As with Greek Christian epitaphs, Latin Christian epitaphs emphasize the separation of the soul from the body and their respective locations under the earth and in Heaven: 'Petronius, you have given your body to the earth but your soul to Christ.'[25]

Moving memorials

Digital death in the form of virtual cemeteries and memorials eliminates the physical barriers for the location and commemoration of the deceased in the perpetuation of the cyberdead.[26] Online memorials may be created at websites such as virtualmemorials.com and legacy.com. Virtual memorials do not replace actual memorials, but rather, allow for the commemoration of the deceased beyond a funeral and the borders of a cemetery. Mobile phone apps such as 'The Mourning Post' use GPS to mark the location of graves so that one can access the site and visit a grave from virtually anywhere.[27] Once a gravesite page is created, the phone user/mourner can add or change the messages and information on the memorial pages – an editing feature that is difficult on actual tombstones, especially if changed frequently. The virtual memorial is similar to a cenotaph in that both commemorate the deceased who is buried elsewhere.

Digital death is not limited to the commemoration of actual persons. Burials and memorials for avatars in Second Life mark the death of the virtual dead and are unique to the legacy of ancient death. The website memoris.com is an online cemetery for avatars that rents digital cemetery plots in a virtual cemetery. These burial plots are as expensive as actual cemetery plots and mausolea. At phasinggrace.blogspot.com, for example, a Second Life cemetery plot is available for rent at £400 per month.

In addition to online memorials, moving memorials commemorate the dead in more than one location – the actual place of burial and wherever the memorial happens to be physically present. The AIDS Memorial Quilt is a moving memorial that commemorates the victims of AIDS all over the world.[28] Each block or section of the 40,000 collected since its creation in 1987 commemorates a victim and serves as an epitaph and symbol of their life. The sheer size of the quilt marks the great number of those who have died from AIDS and often only portions of the entire quilt can be displayed.

Moving memorials insert death into the urban fabric by blending epitaphs amidst the signage of traffic signs, billboards, and retail store signage that may themselves be the surface on which memorial murals are painted, such as murals in all five boroughs of New York City that commemorate the victims of 9/11.[29] White 'ghost bikes' on pavements near the place where a cyclist was killed are both shrines and safety warnings.[30] The memorials are effective since they evoke the common urban sight of bikes locked to signposts, but with flowers, messages, and other items to indicate that the cyclist will not return to unlock the bike. Other memorials are viewed while they are moving through the urban centre. The Georgia Law Enforcement Moving Memorial Wall, for example, lists the names of more than 600 officers killed in the line of duty.[31] Their names appear on the sides of a trailer that travels with a motorcycle escort of the Georgia Blue Knights.

Decals, usually affixed to the rear window of an automobile, are moving tombstone memorials that travel with the commemorator. Memorial designs vary but a common decal message includes the phrase 'Rest in Peace' and gives the name and birth/death dates of the deceased. Decals with the picture of a deceased pet are also common. This removal of epitaphs from the cemetery to the automobile of the commemorator further removes the dead from the periphery. From a figurative standpoint, automobiles that convey memorials to the deceased offer a variation of a hearse that conveys the actual body of the deceased through the urban core of city or town. In the case of the decal, however, the moving tombstone alludes to a burial already completed and marked with the original epitaph.

CULT OF THE DEAD

Tattoos are another form of moving memorial that turns the bodies of commemorators into human memorials. In addition to the completed tattoo, the physical pain involved in the application of the tattoo is considered part of the grieving process in overcoming the emotional loss of the death. The tattoo keeps the memory (and portrait depending on the design) of the deceased as close as possible as it celebrates the life of the deceased to those who read it.[32] The disposal of the body of someone with a memorial tattoo represents multiple layers of commemoration – a body that is itself marked with the commemoration of another person who predeceased them.

Related to tattoos are memorial t-shirts. The design may be similar to those of automobile decals and tattoos and include a portrait, biographical details, and a message to the deceased. All of these forms of moving memorials represent the wearing of a memorial, but jewellery with cremated remains, rather than just the name of the deceased, represents the actual wearing of the dead, and redefines mourning jewellery, whether black pieces or Victorian mourning rings containing strands of hair of a deceased loved one, worn by a woman in mourning.[33] Only a small portion of the cremated remains can be stored in the necklace containers so the deceased is literally stored in multiple containers. When not being worn, the memorial necklace may be stored in the home and placed in a glass display case.

Visiting the dead

Although the home may serve as a complementary site for the commemoration of the dead with its shared memories and mementos of the deceased, the primary site of remembrance of the dead is the grave. The act of burial, whether by inhumation, in an ossuary, or the storage of cremated remains literally situates the dead at a site that comes with a title with which the dead take possession of the tomb. The site or cemetery plot numbers that serve as street address extend the metaphor of visiting or calling on the dead. A sense of ownership of the grave may complement an owned home or contrast with a rented apartment. The completed site with flowers, shrubs, and statuary evokes a landscaped garden or a rooftop terrace with the living quarters below.

The two locations, however, have more in common than being the former and current homes of the deceased.[34] On the day of burial, families often gather at the home for a ritual meal or for prayer such as during the *shivah* – morning and evening prayers held in the home in the week following an Orthodox Jewish funeral. On future visits to the cemetery, the bringing of flowers, gifts, cards, candles and other items parallel the bringing of gifts when visiting someone's home. In the case of memorials with portraits of then living family members in mourning or performing a funerary ritual, such as the Staglieno Cemetery tombs of the Pienovi (Chapter I/ Fig. 1); Gallino (Chapter III/Fig. 12), and Piaggio families (Chapter III/Fig. 22), a visit to the grave as the home of the dead becomes one that is also figuratively full of family members who are frozen in age and time (like those whose bedrooms have become shrines). Both the home and the site of burial serve as the backdrop for the expression and the (re)experience of grief.

The leaving of flowers or other mementos, the tending or cleaning the gravestone or site, or the placing of a stone for Jewish burials all represent repeat rituals at the site of burial. A well-tended gravesite is like the tending of home gardens and serves as evidence for continued commemoration (or neglect) of the dead, as a reflection of the morality condition of the living. The Qingming, Ancestors' Day, or Chinese Tomb Sweeping Day, is a public outdoor holiday that takes place on the 15th day from the Spring Equinox (usually around April 5th). It is customary for family members to tend to the graves and to make dry food offerings. Tomb cleaning is also observed by members of the Greek Orthodox Church. The dead may be included to mark religious observances such as Muslim pilgrims visiting the graves of loved ones ahead of Ramadan. The growing of flowers at home to plant at the grave further connects the two locations, literally and figuratively.[35] The social connection to these activities and objects adds to the symbolism and increases the level of affection and expression of grief.

In ancient Greece, propitiating offerings of libations (*choai*) of honey, milk, water, wine, and oil that may be followed by the blood of an animal sacrificed over the grave, and meals, were made at the grave on the 3rd, 9th and 30th days, and one year later, but it is unclear whether the dates are reckoned from the date of death or burial. Little is known about the types of food left at the grave for the dead but honey cake (*melitoutta*), an egg or a favourite meal are attested to.[36] Unlike Romans, Greeks did not eat meals with the dead at the grave. In Athens, the 30th-day rites seem to mark the end of the obsequies. Other occasions on which Athenians made grave offerings were at the festivals of the *Genesia* (September) and family commemorative days, such as birthdays. The festival of the *Anthesteria* (Spring) was devoted to the dead collectively but it did not involve visits to the gravesites of dead ancestors.[37]

A feature of archaic Greek burials is the (re)viewing of the dead in scenes of *prothesis* that appear at the place of burial on grave markers visible to visitors.[38] Among grave markers in Attic cemeteries, kraters were half-buried to mark the place of burial and to provide a vessel for the pouring of graveside libations [**Fig. 2**]. Scenes of *prothesis* and lamentation are depicted on kraters and plaques that appear above ground and mark the site of burial, but they also commemorate mourning activities that occurred prior to burial. This 'display of the displaying of the dead' on an object also results in the 'viewing of the viewing of the dead' by a graveside visitor/spectator and offers a temporal transposition of the former visitation and mourning with the current burial of the deceased. Depicted scenes of mourning are those that occurred before committal/burial rather than scenes of a committal/burial. To later generations subject to more strict funerary laws, these archaic scenes of vibrant and public mourning may also represent a symbolic defiance of contemporary laws and a reminder of the previous public roles of women in funerary ritual.[39]

Past and present blend in successive visits to the tomb in repeated viewing of the krater or plaque, whose scenes of mourning have not changed since the last visit, and which continued even in the absence of any viewers/mourners. The displaying and viewing of past scenes of visitation and lamentation at the site of burial also represent a continuation of mourning into the future. Family members will see representations of mourning on each visit; such scenes are being played out even when they are not physically present between visits. This perpetual tending of the dead may be a comfort to those who do not want to leave the dead alone between their visits to the grave but also when they inevitably die themselves at which time, they may want a similar grave marker to ensure that they themselves are not forgotten.

Vases (*lekythoi*) from the Classical period used exclusively for sacrificial offerings at the graveside in Athens depict personifications of figures associated with death but also stylized scenes of funerals: the *prothesis*, *ekphora*, and figures visiting the grave to mourn or to make offerings of libations or leave garlands.[40] Actual mourners who had mirrored those same actions during the funeral left these vases as grave goods. Once at the grave, however, the acts of *prothesis* and *ekphora* were over, but the rite of grave offerings was in progress during burial. Since the vases were buried with the deceased after ritual libation, the depiction of the offering was afterwards lost from view, thus giving finality to the burial and the initial grave offerings: actual and depicted funeral activities are over. The fugitive quality of the paint that was used on the vases further anticipated and symbolized this finality. In other words, the mourner walks away from the grave where they made offerings to the deceased with a vase that depicted a representation of their former roles as mourners holding a *prothesis*, participating in the procession, or making grave offerings.

These images on sacrificial vases are symbolic of funerary ritual but their depiction on actual funerary markers represents perennial mourning prior to burial at the place of burial or at the site of cremated remains. Mourning that was held indoors during the visitation continues (figuratively) outdoors after the conclusion of the funeral. The effect is to present a visual recreation of the deceased's funeral at the place of burial where the events that commenced the obsequies are represented at the place where they ended. The ritual cycle of visitation, burial, commemoration, and cult of the dead is at odds with the representation of one element from that cycle at the place where another element took place. The representations of deceased and mourner seem to contradict the fact of burial as it reaffirms the acts of mourning, for the present but also in the future. The lack of scenes depicting burials at the place of burial implies a desire to extend and to commemo-rate mourning rather than to re-experience the act of burial itself.

Drinking and eating with the dead

In ancient Rome, liquid and food offerings were made at graves and ritual meals were shared between the living and the dead. These funeral and death commemoration rituals erased the figurative and actual boundaries between the living and the dead even as it perpetuated an identity for the dead with whom the living maintained an ongoing relationship. The offering of food, whether on the pyre or at the grave, was an important part of the cult of the dead but sources are silent whether food offerings were as elaborate as the meals associated with the Mexican Day of the Dead *ofrendas* (see below) or those left at Chinese graves.[41]

For Romans, these ritual acts were not merely symbolic. Lucian, in his essay *On Funerals*, describes the dependency of the thirsty and hungry dead on the drink and food offerings of the living (9):

> But those of the middle way of life [neither virtuous or vicious], and they are many, wander about in the meadow [of the Underworld] without their bodies, in the form of shadows that vanish like smoke in your fingers. They get their nourishment, naturally, from the liba-tions that are poured in our world and the burnt-offerings at the tomb; so that if anyone has not left a friend or kinsman behind him on earth, he goes about his business there as an unfed corpse, in a state of famine.[42]

Lucian's essay is critical of superstitious beliefs of the afterlife but his description of Greek, Etruscan, and Roman rituals associated with the cult of the dead appear to reflect popular views and practices borne out by pipes at gravesites, ritual meals, funerary monuments, including sarcophagi and urns, and epitaphs, written in the ostensible voice of the deceased, that state they receive nourishment from libations and sacrifices.[43] An epitaph found

Fig. 25. Funerary Altar of Attia Agele. Museo Chiaramonti, Vatican Museums.

in Rome asks a passer-by to share wine with the deceased: 'If you are a pleasant man, mix (wine), drink and give (it) to me.'[44]

Funerary art also reflects the importance of food and drink to the cult of the dead. A scene from Tomb 17–18 in the Via Laurentina Necropolis, that dates to the late first century BCE, for example, shows the deceased reclining on a couch (*kline*)with his wife seated in front of him next to a table with food.[45] The funerary altar of Attia Agele in the Museo Chiaramonti, Vatican Museums [**Fig. 25**] depicts the deceased reclining on a *kline* holding a cup with other vessels on a table.[46] The sarcophagus of Caecilius Vallianus in the Museo Gregorio Profano, Vatican Museums, shows the deceased reclining on a couch surrounded by erotes/puti as servants bring both cooked and raw food and wine to his table.[47] The presence of trees and flowers suggests an outdoor meal, possibly an allusion to a funeral banquet at the site of his monument at which he joins those commemorating him.

In ancient Rome, unlike the Greek meal that followed burial and was eaten in the home (*perideipnon*), grave offerings to the dead were just as important as meals eaten with the dead at the site of burial.[48] On the day of the funeral, a ritual meal called the *silicernium* was eaten at the tomb that may have included the consumption of sausage.[49] A graveside meal was repeated nine days after burial, called the *cena novemdialis*, which may be related to the meal consumed at Greek tombs nine days after burial. This ritual marked the end of the mourning period and consisted of libations and a sacrifice to the Manes of the deceased prior to the consumption of a meal. Menu items were fixed by tradition: eggs, vegetables, beans, lentils and salt, bread, and poultry.[50] Food was also left at the tomb for the deceased that, if stolen and eaten, would incur pollution. These rituals point to a belief that the spirit of the deceased resided in the tomb that was considered a *domus aeterna*, or eternal home, even as belief in the Underworld would suggest a collective home among all the dead. Shrines in the home called the *lararium* were devoted to the household gods (*lares, penates*) but included representations (*imagines*) of ancestors, signalling the reintegration of the dead (*manes*) in the home of survivors. Following the funeral ceremonies on the day of burial and nine days later, meals with the dead were repeated on commemorative feast days.

In addition to rites associated with funerals, the Roman calendar contained annual festivals dedicated to the cult of the dead. The *Parentalia* that took place from February 13th to the 21st was dedicated to the commemoration of ancestors. The last day of the *Parentalia* was called the Feralia and was dedicated to the city-wide worship of the Manes. The *Rosalia*, the feast of roses, took place in May and June;[51] and the *Lemuria*, held on May 9th, 11th, and 13th, was apotropaic in nature and involved the voicing of incantations to ward off the dead.

On the occasion of the *Parentalia*, liquid offerings could be made to the dead at tombs, often directly into pipes or mosaic floors with holes made for the pouring of libations for the thirsty and hungry dead.[52] As with Greek ritual that prescribed the pouring of liquids such as wine, oils, and perfumes from *lekythoi*, slender urns specifically made to contain funeral libations, Roman funerary rites also prescribed specific vessels for the offering of libations, a pitcher and *patera* or platter. These ritual implements are often depicted on Roman funerary altars, such as the tomb of Cominia Tyche, which dates to the Flavian or Trajanic period, and is now in the Metropolitan Museum of Art, NY. Like representations of prothesis and ekphora scenes on pottery and plaques at the site of burial that depict events prior to burial, the pitcher and a *patera* for the offering of libations are representations of the actual instruments used for graveside liquid offerings. Rather than being prescriptive of ritual, however, the depiction of vessels suggests perpetual observance of the rites in evocation of their first performance on the day of the funeral.

In other cases, epitaphs on funerary and commemorative monuments specify that on the occasion of the *Parentalia,* the birthday of the deceased or some other occasion, a feast or monetary gift would be given in perpetuity to those commemorating the deceased.[53] Repeated performance of the rites ensured the perpetuation of the identity and memory of the deceased. Literary descriptions of the performance of graveside rites, such as Catullus 101 in which he visits the tomb of his brother, and the *Aeneid* Book 5 in which Aeneas offers libations at the grave of his father Anchises, elicit pathos through the performance of the rites. Contributing to the pathos of the scenes, however, is the realization on the parts of the performer of the rites and the reader, that the rites will not be repeated due to the vast distance of the graves from the homes of survivors. Ausonius' *Parentalia* is a collection of ostensible verse epitaphs dedicated to family members, that evoke a stroll amidst their graves in evocation of the *Parentalia* rites. Unlike the descriptions of rites in Catullus and Vergil, the reader participates, rather than merely observes in the rites. The reading of the poems serves as allusion and substitution of the ritual, thus perpetuating the commemoration of Ausonius' family members.[54]

Representations of the drinking dead are found inside tombs (see Chapter III for frescoes of banqueting in Etruscan tombs) and on funerary monuments. The scenes seems less exuberant than the Etruscan painting of banqueting and dancing but the memorialisation of the deceased in a banquet setting shares much with the earlier tradition of funerary art and shows the enduring tradition of drinking in the tomb. A fresco from Columbarium 31 in the Via Laurentina Necropolis, Ostia Antica (now in the Vatican Museums) that dates to the first half of the third century CE, depicts banqueters at a meal in honour of the dead.[55] The columbarium was built with three dining couches situated below niches that held cremation urns and this painting. The banqueters' names appear above each figure and seem typical of freedmen (Felix, Foebus, and Fortunatus). The banqueters, dressed in white tunics and cloaks, recline on a semi-circular couch (*sigma* or *stibadium*) and may commemorate a ritual meal held in honour of one of the columbarium's occupants who may have been a member of the same corporation or funeral club.[56] The painting may also serve as a substitution of ritual when family and friends are no longer alive to commemorate the dead.

Funerary food rituals were also incorporated into cemetery and tomb design, such as tombs with stone dining couches for al fresco dining or at communal dining areas at a cemetery or catacombs. As with roadside memorials and necropolis tombs, urbanization has largely destroyed the evidence for communal dining areas along Roman roads and in Roman cemeteries.[57] Archaeological evidence survives outside of Rome, however, where tombs with stone dining couches at the entrance are preserved or have been documented, such as those at Isola Sacra Necropolis and Pompeii at so-called house tombs (Chapter III).[58] Along a stretch of the road that leads out of Ostia Antica are the remains of 100 tombs of various design and size. Of the tombs that survive at Isola Sacra, 14 were built with two stone dining couches, or *biclinia*, on either side of the entrance and 3 with three stone dining couches, or *triclinia*.[59] The entrance to Tomb 15 (attributed to Verria Zosime but the inscription may come from Tomb 29) is flanked by stone couches that would have been used for ritual meals associated with the cult of the dead [**Fig. 26**]. Tomb 80 was built in conjunction with Tombs 77–79, each of which was equipped with *biclinia* couches at the entrances to the tombs with a square brick base for a table. Meals were not prepared off-site and packed picnic-style, but rather, ovens and wells were located in the vicinity of these *biclinia* tombs for the preparation of meals.

Fig. 26. Tomb 15. Isola Sacra/Portus Necropolis.

Modern variations of drinking and eating with the dead extend the traditional Irish wake in which the deceased is mourned in their home during visitation by visitors who drink in their honour.[60] The 'Big Mama's Kitchen' theme funeral at the Wade Funeral Home, St. Louis, MO (Chapter 1) offers an institutionalised version of visiting the home of the deceased for their wake for a vibrant, rather than a sombre, wake experience. A set that is designed to look like a kitchen with a refrigerator, stove, and kitchen table is set up inside a traditional funeral parlour room. Mourner/guests are invited to pull up to the table that is situated close to the coffin and eat gumbo that is boiling on the stove or pies that are baking in the oven. The deceased (re)assumes the role of 'Big Mama.' The role-playing erases the figurative boundaries between the living and the dead and gives women choosing this theme funeral an opportunity to entertain guests in their kitchen even in death. Mourners, in turn, leave the funeral home as though leaving Mama's kitchen for a final time.

Like ancient Rome, the cemetery may also form the backdrop to meals with the dead. Antoinette K-Doe sat next to an effigy of her husband Ernie at his tomb in St. Louis Cemetery No. 2 in New Orleans, LA and served gumbo and soft drinks under a tent to cemetery visitors on All Saints' Day. The same effigy of her husband had sat in the driver's seat of the carriage that transported his coffin to the cemetery (Chapter I). For the rest of the calendar year, the effigy was a familiar fixture in the lounge The Mother-in-Law, owned by Antoinette, where he sat on a throne among club patrons.

In addition to tombs, meals and banquets could be held in other locations in ancient Rome such as columbaria and catacombs and structures that were common in the suburbs such as *cellae, memoriae, exedrae*, and *scholae*, which were used for feasts by the relatives and friends of people buried underneath them.[61] These facilities could be outfitted with cabinets and supplies needed for banquets such as lamps, vessels, pillows and cloaks. Christians also participated in funereal banquets and an area for communal funereal banquets was also incorporated into catacombs. At the Catacombs of San Sebastiano, Rome, for example, the 'Triglia' was an open-air space that was the site of the so-called love feast (*Agape*). The space was in use in the late third and early fourth century CE until it was covered over during construction of the Basilica under which it lies, roughly in the centre. Hundreds of graffiti that were left by the banqueters line the walls.

The logistics involved in the gathering of family members and friends at tombs to eat a meal on the same day may begin en route since the normal considerations in effect for walking to/from tombs since crowds would be on the roads to make the journey to the graves of loved ones. The distances travelled to the various tombs and monuments along the roads leading into/out of Rome could be considerably further than the distance for an Athenian to travel to the Kerameikos or Dipylon cemeteries (Chapter III). The convergence of relatives at the same site on the same day who would require facilities for the preparation of meals and places to eat may also have been a factor, especially on feast days.[62] Today, it would be difficult to imagine every tomb in any given cemetery being visited at the same time, but crowds preparing and eating food at the entrances of tombs at the same time would suggest high levels of traffic, odour, and noise resembling dinner-time outside of tents in assigned spots at camping grounds.

Grave gardens were also the literal and figurative settings for meals with the dead. A grave garden (*cepotaphium*) belonged legally to the deceased for the harvesting of wine and fruit to supply the food for an annual commemorative meal for survivors who would dine at the site of the grave garden. The epitaph of the freedman Gaius Hostius Pamphilus (CIL 6.9583) identifies the main occupants and other (extended) family members who will continue their associations in death. The inscription also gives physical details about the orchards surrounding the grave:

> Gaius Hostius Pamphilus freedman of Gaius,
> a doctor, bought this monument for himself,
> for Nelpia Hymnis the freedwoman of Marcus,
> and for all of their freedmen and their descendants.
> This is our eternal home, this is our farm,
> these our gardens, and this is our memorial.
> Frontage 13 feet, depth 24 feet.[63]

An epitaph from Langres, France that dates to late first or early second century CE illustrates the extent to which some sought to control their own cult after death. It is clear in this epitaph that the deceased retains his role as host to ritual meals in extraordinary lavishness:

> My wishes are that the memorial shrine should be completed according to the plan I left. The shrine is to contain a recess, in which there is to be put a seated statue of myself, made of the finest imported marble or else of the best bronze, at least 5 feet in height. Just inside the recess there is to be a couch, with two seats on either side of it, all made from imported marble. There are to be covers kept there, which are to be spread out on the days when the memorial shrine is opened, and there are to be two rugs, two dining cushions of equal size, two woollen cloaks and a tunic. In front of this building is to be placed an altar, carved with the finest decoration from the best Luna marble, and in this my bones are to rest. The shrine is to be

closed with a slab of Luna marble, in such a way that it can be both easily opened and shut again. The care of the shrine and the orchards and ponds is to be supervised by my freedmen Philadelphus and Verus, and money shall be supplied for rebuilding and repairs should any of these suffer damage or destruction. There are to be three landscape gardeners and their apprentices, and if one or more of them die or are removed others are to be substituted in their place.[64]

It is impossible to say the extent to which the deceased's wishes were carried out and for how long. The details of the tomb's appearance, the supplies that are to be on hand for annual festivals, and the staff to maintain the shrine and landscaped gardens suggest that at least, initially, the tomb and surrounding gardens were maintained as prescribed by the epitaph.

Ancient accounts of graveside rituals that were imitated in the dining rooms allude to and subvert actual rituals, such as the self-representation of the host as an entertaining corpse at dinner parties in subversive reenactments of the *Parentalia*. Pacuvius, Governor of Syria, held infamous *carpe diem* dinner parties on a regular basis according to Seneca who condemns such behaviour (*Epistle* 12.8–9):

Pacuvius, who from habit made Syria his own, with wine and funeral feasts commemorated himself (*parentaverat*), thus he was carried into his room from the dinner table, while, among the applause of boys, this was sung to the accompaniment of music: 'He lived, he lived.' Not just on this one day was he carried out to burial.

In playing dead, apparently on multiple occasions, Pacuvius commemorates himself, thus performing the roles of corpse and mourner simultaneously. As host, Pacuvius turns his dinner party into a funereal banquet.[65] The role-playing extends to the servants and dinner guests who also assume the roles of mourner and commemorator.

Pacuvius recalls the subversive allusion to the *Parentalia* by the freedman Trimalchio in Petronius' *Satyricon*. In the course of a dinner party, Trimalchio is carried into the dining room and later pre-enacts his funeral as he lays himself out as a corpse before his initially unwitting guests. But as the meal progresses, he goes further by asking his guests/mourners to imagine themselves at his *Parentalia* (78.4) thus turning his mock funeral into a prelude of the commemoration of his death and funeral during the *Parentalia*. The guests and his household are turned into mourners whose performances at the mock funeral will be rewarded after his actual funeral. The mistaking of his funeral music for a fire alarm that brings the fire brigade smashing their way into the dining room breaks the dramatic illusion and allusion to the ritual. The episode exemplifies Trimalchio's manipulation of his guests and Petronius' manipulation of his readers who realize that the dinner itself was a funeral banquet in honour of Trimalchio.

A terrifying example of alluding to the cult of the dead at a dinner party, however, can be found in the 'Black Dinner' given by the Emperor Domitian. The evocation was as eerie as the uncertainty as to the Emperor's message by his evocation. According to the historian Dio (*Epitome* 57.9), Domitian invited prominent senators and knights to dinner that was held in an entirely black room that evoked a tomb. Gravestones inscribed with the names of guests and tomb lamps were placed near each guest who reclined on funeral couches. Boys painted black assumed the roles of the guests' death spirits and sat at their feet as black funeral offerings and sacrifices were served to the guests on black dishes. The emperor alternated between deadly silence and conversation about death as though the guests were already among the dead. After the dinner, the tombstone and other dinner serving pieces were brought to the homes of the guests who were expecting imminent death. As though to signal their return to life, however, the boys who had been painted black as their death spirits returned washed and dressed in white.

Dio's account has been interpreted as a misunderstood part of his triumphal festivities for his triumph over the Dacians or as an anticipation of the *Parentalia* but it appears that the dinner is a *Parentalia* in progress.[66] Rather than commemorate the dead, the guests are forced to participate in their own death ritual. The temporal transposition of (self-) commemoration in a funerary ritual prior to death imposes a self-identification with the dead onto the guests by the emperor who is himself not subject to death. The subversion of the *Parentalia* at the banquet seems to have satisfied the sadistic appetite of Domitian at the expense of his terrified guests, who commemorated themselves at a funereal banquet as though dead all the while anticipating their own actual deaths.

Traditional European visits to the grave are sombre events. In William Adolph Bouguereau's painting 'Le Jour des Morts' (1859), for example, two grieving widows dressed in black kneel before an unmarked grave holding wreaths. The scene is one of Romantic external expression of grief. The emphasis is on the younger woman who kneels seeking the support of the older woman. She does not wear a veil but her face is turned towards the older woman and away from the viewer's gaze. The timeless landscape suggests the universality of grief. The formality of the scene contrasts with the festive atmosphere of modern Day of the Dead celebrations.

The modern Day of the Dead festival removes figurative barriers between the living and the dead and, like the *Parentalia*, provides an opportunity for lively on-going social relationship with the dead.[67] The Festival takes place over two days: the first day, on November first, All Saints' Day, is devoted to deceased children and infants. The second day, November 2nd, corresponds to the Catholic All Souls' Day. Mexican, Latin and South American festivals of the Day(s) of the Dead are called *El Día de los Muertos*.[68] In addition to prayers for the souls of the deceased, *ofrenda* of food and drink are offered at graves and home altars that consist of flowers, candles, breads, candies, fruits, vegetables, in particular squash, and other cooked food items such as tamales and chicken or turkey *mole*. The prominence of sugar and sweetened food items, such as sweet bread offerings on graves, is a particular feature of *ofrenda* that can be traced back to Day of the Dead celebrations (*Día de los Difuntos*) in Spain since the 1500s.

The Day of the Dead is a festive celebration of parties and parades that is reflected in the images of dancing skeletons and mariachi bands. The popularity of skeleton masks and costumes of bride and groom skeletons point to the growing convergence of North American Halloween and Day of the Dead celebrations that threaten the latter as a distinct Mexican tradition.[69] The repopulation of homes and cities with the figurative dancing dead contrasts with the literal drinking and dancing with the dead in Madagascar during the *famadihana* (literally 'turning of bones') rite celebration. Every five or seven years, the bodies of the dead are exhumed or removed from family crypts. The bodies, wrapped in shrouds, are sprayed with perfume or wine and are lifted by family members who dance with them held high above their shoulders for several hours before returning them to their tombs.

Touring the dead

Modern tourism centred on cemeteries and religious sites for the tombs of religious, political, or famous celebrities, and on museum exhibitions that focus on burial and funeral customs, turn private visits to the graves of loved ones into public and spiritual visits to culturally significant sites and memorials associated with disposal and funerary ritual. Tourist and pilgrim visits to places of burial (actual or recreated in museums) are distinct from haunted tours or dark tourism that is centred on the actual site of death.[70] The cemetery as open-air museum with funerary monuments as works of art, such as Staglieno Cemetery, Genoa, Campo Verano Cemetery, Rome and the Protestant Cemetery, Rome, and is literally a visit to a museum at Forest Lawn Cemetery, which contains a museum with rotating exhibitions.[71] Pilgrimages to tombs of major religious significance include the Cave of the Patriarchs in Hebron, where Jewish, Christian, and Islamic tradition places the tombs of Adam and Eve, and the family of Abraham; the Tomb of Jesus in the Church of the Holy Sepulchre, the tomb of the Prophet Muhammad in the Al-Masjid al-Nabawi Mosque in Medina, Saudi Arabia; and Christian martyr shrines, such as St. Peter's Basilica and the Basilica of S. Sebastiano ad Catacumbas, which were built over the tombs of their namesakes and other martyrs (Chapter III).

Pilgrimages to the tombs of famous Greeks and Romans were also common in antiquity. Among burial monuments that were visited for their grandeur, such as the Great Egyptian Pyramids at Giza and the Tomb of

Achilles, the Mausoleum of Mausolus in Halicarnassus, the Tomb of Alexander the Great in Alexandria – the namesake of the mausoleum and one of the seven ancient wonders of the world – stands out for its political significance to Roman generals and dynasts such as Pompey the Great, Julius Caesar, and the Emperor Augustus.[72] In 215 CE, the Emperor Caracalla made the last recorded visit to the tomb and looked upon the embalmed Alexander, who was amazingly well preserved.[73] In addition to being an act of devotion to the great military leader, these visits ensured that the military successes of the visitors would be framed in relation to Alexander's. Since Rome's empire extended over the regions conquered by Alexander, the tomb also symbolized Alexander's death and the potential for even greater military glory by the generals who were still achieving glory.

Modern visits to the tombs of famous political leaders continue, often at sites that are designed to accommodate large crowds of tourists. The grave of President John F. Kennedy at Arlington National Cemetery, for example, is approached by special paths and designed with a marble elliptical plaza to allow for crowd circulation. The plaza design evokes the traditional *ambulacrum* of basilica apses that allowed for the viewing of relics by pilgrims who would walk past in an orderly manner. Although famous memorials had been consulted, including the Mausoleum of Halicarnassus, the final design is of a simple grave with an eternal flame, in front of Arlington House, the Robert E. Lee Memorial (also known as Custis-Lee Mansion) that is aligned with the Washington Monument and the Lincoln Memorial, and also includes the graves of Jacqueline Kennedy Onassis and their two children who died in infancy. The visitor centre at the cemetery and the Kennedy grave attracts tens of thousands of tourists daily.

Vergil's tomb was among the famous ancient monuments and sites visited on the 'Grand Tour' from the seventeenth to nineteenth centuries.[74] The exact location of Vergil's grave is unknown but it became associated with a columbarium next to the tunnel on Mount Posillipo (also known as Crypta Neapolitana, Grotta di Posillipo, Grotta Vecchia) that connected Naples to Baiae, Cumae, and Pozzuoli. The history of the tomb is as interesting as the history of the dead Vergil. The poet Silius Italicus bought the tomb/land (as he had with Cicero's Tusculan estate) and worshipped at Vergil's tomb on his birthday.[75] Silius' devotion is the subject of Joseph Wright of Derby's painting, 'Silius Italicus at Vergil's tomb, 1779' and is one of many paintings and prints that depict the tomb in a romanticised landscape.

Vergil's tomb became the renewed focus of attention in the twelfth century when supernatural powers were attributed to Vergil's remains. The bones were subsequently moved to Castel dell' Ovo in the early thirteenth century for the safety of Neapolitans after they refused to give them to the Englishman Gervase of Tilbury, who was granted permission by Roger the Norman to take possession of the contents of the tomb. They did, however, allow him to take a book of magic that was placed under Vergil's head, a detail that is odd since Vergil had been cremated. In the fourteenth-century, interest in the dead Vergil continued: Petrarch visited the grave and Vergil guides Dante through Hell and Purgatory in the *Divine Comedy*. After centuries of being visited and memorialized in paintings and prints, the Fascists continued the appropriation of the dead Vergil and the literary/topographic history of the site by relocating the remains of the Italian Romantic poet Giacomo Leopardi at Vergil's tomb. This makes explicit the connection between Vergil and Leopardi and Imperial Rome and Fascist Rome but also the appropriation of Romantic poetry and the tomb's romanticized landscape from visitors on the Grand Tour.

Exhibitions that display or tour the dead differ from exhibitions on the history of funerary culture, which take visitors behind the scenes of the funeral industry and funeral homes to exhibit both the process and instruments, from embalming to funeral processions.[76] Visitors to museums see Egyptian or Incan mummies behind a glass case, often with funerary objects that were found at the time of the mummy's discovery.[77] The King Tut exhibition 'The Treasures of Tutankhamun' that toured from 1972 to 1979 was a blockbuster show that became a part of American pop culture with comedian Steve Martin's song 'King Tut'. Millions of people attended the exhibition, which included his famous gold mask, including more than eight million at The Metropolitan Museum of Art, New York, which organised the US exhibition. The most recent exhibition, 'Tutankhamun and the Golden Age of the Pharoahs' is currently touring with objects from King Tutankhamun's predecessors and objects from his own tomb which have not been previously displayed.

The public interest in viewing ancient corpses has a long tradition.[78] The discovery and display of the preserved body of a young woman variously identified (so-called 'Tulliola') whose sarcophagus was found on the Via Appia in 1485 created a sensation (Chapter I).[79] Visitors were amazed at the supple quality of her skin and body parts that were apparently repeatedly tested, since only after the removal of the preservative did the flesh begin to discolour. Various contemporary accounts survive.[80] According to Celio Rodigino, Leandro Alberti, Alexander ab Alexandro, and Corona:

> The body is described as well arranged in the coffin, with arms and legs still flexible. The hair was blonde, and bound by a fillet (*infula*) woven of gold. The colour of the flesh was absolutely lifelike. The eyes and mouth were partly open, and if one drew the tongue out slightly it would go back to its place of itself. During the first days of the exhibition on the Capitol this wonderful relic showed no signs of decay; but after a time the action of the air began to tell upon it, and the face and hands turned black. The coffin seems to have been placed near the cistern of the Conservatori palace, so as to allow the crowd of visitors to move around and behold the wonder with more ease. Celio Rodigino says that the first symptoms of putrefaction were noticed on the third day; and he attributes the decay more to the removal of the coating of ointments than to the action of the air.

Other contemporary sources describe the great interest in the exhibition of the girl. From a letter dated to the day of the discovery: 'Words cannot describe the number and the excitement of the multitudes who rushed to admire this marvel. To make matters easy, the Conservatori have agreed to remove the beautiful body to the Capitol. One would think there is some great indulgence and remission of sins to be gained by climbing that hill, so great is the

crowd, especially of women, attracted by the sight.' According to Daniele da
San Sebastiano in a letter also dated to 1485, 'The eyelids could be opened
and shut; the ears and the nose were so well preserved that, after being bent
to one side or the other, they instantly resumed their original shape. By pressing
the flesh of the cheeks the colour would disappear as in a living body. The
tongue could be seen through the pink lips; the articulations of the hands
and feet still retained their elasticity. The whole of Rome, men and women,
to the number of twenty thousand, visited the marvel of Santa Maria Nova
that day.' Unlike her body, the fame of the young woman was short-lived. It
is believed that her body was either unceremoniously dumped into the Tiber
or buried outside the Porta Salaria by order of Pope Innocent VIII who
sought to quell popular excitement and superstition.

The exhibiting of a corpse whose place of burial was disturbed also
includes the display of the mummified bodies of Henri IV and Henri de
La Tour d'Auvergne, vicomte de Turenne (1611–1675) following the govern-
ment-sanctioned destruction of tombs in 1793 during the French
Revolution.[81] Since the bodies of Turenne and Henri IV were in a remarkable state of preservation (unlike other royal bodies that were thrown into
pits outside the Basilica), they were displayed in the Royal Necropolis of
the Cathedral Basilica of Saint-Denis, where spectators touched and muti-
lated the bodies. Turenne's well-preserved body and his military service to
France were seen as moral merits, and helped it escape the vandalism and
desecration meted out to the other occupants of the Royal Necropolis. For
about five years, Turenne's body was displayed at the Jardin des Plantes as
part of the Muséum d'Histoire Naturelle among natural history exhibits
where spectators could continue to touch his mummified remains. Alexandre
Lenoir moved Turenne's monumental pyramid tomb (Chapter III) from
Saint-Denis to the garden cemetery (Jardin Élysée) that was adjacent to
his Musée des Monuments Français in which he finally interred the mummy
out of public view. Napoleon later translated Turenne's remains and moved
his tomb to Temple de Mars (now Les Invalides).[82] The head of Henri IV
circulated in private collections but was recently identified by scientists and
returned to one of his descendants.[83]

In addition to Turenne's tomb, Alexandre Lenoir's 'Museum of French Monuments' displayed (and saved) many other royal funerary monuments (from the twelfth to sixteenth centuries) from the Cathedral Basilica of Saint-Denis royal necropolis, at first spontaneously ransacked during the French Revolution but whose monuments and buried bodies were later destroyed and desecrated by government sanction under the supervision of Lenoir).[84] Lenoir, for example, received a bayonet thrust in saving Cardinal Richelieu's embalmed face from mutilation by those trying to destroy his tomb. Lenoir claimed that the tombs were art not tombs and they were displayed in the Jardin Élysée. The museum first opened in 1793 and was given the official name of Musée des Antiquités et Monuments Français in 1796. The art pieces including funerary monuments, however, were returned to their original owners or to Saint-Denis by decree of Louis XVIII in 1816. Since the tombs no longer contained bodies, the Royal Necropolis had itself become a museum of funerary monuments, with Les Invalides taking its place as the burial monument of the French Republic. Lenoir's Museum followed the opening of the Palazzo Nuovo, designed by Michelangelo as part of the Capitoline Museums during the Pontificate of Clement XII to house famous ancient statuary. The halls and galleries are lined with epigraphs, including funeral markers (*tituli*) amidst the sculpture, some of which is funereal, like the Flavian Woman as Venus.[85] Today, the Galleria Congiunzione that connects the Palazzo Nuovo to the Palazzo dei Conservatori (below the Piazza di Campidoglio) contains cinerary urns and funerary markers as part of the Galleria Lapidaria collection that expands the display space of *tituli*.

What happens when a museum becomes the burial location of the contemporary deceased rather than the display place of ancient funerary art and corpses? Survivors of 9/11 are facing this unique dilemma with the construction of the National September 11 Memorial and Museum that will also serve as a tomb and memorial of 9/11 victims. This conflation of identities and purposes associated with the site means that visitors will have multiple and varying reactions to the various elements of the site: family members visiting the place of death, grave and memorial of loved ones and visitors to the museum and memorial paying their respects and contextu-alizing the events and consequences of 9/11. Although the museum and memorial commemorate all of the victims of 9/11, the site marks the loca-tion where victims were killed, thus some visits may also be considered examples of 'dark tourism', adding further concerns to survivors of the public and private functions of the memorial. The construction of the new Freedom Tower contributes to the complexity of the site as sacred commemorative space and a commercial hub, recalling the former World Trade Center Towers, and also conveys messages of political and personal strength and survival.

At the 10-year anniversary mark, emotions are still raw as survivors are confronted with the loss of loved ones and the questions of where and how they are being commemorated, with some family members calling for an above-ground location distinct from the museum.[86] Words and word place-ment on the memorial are equally important. The placement of names on the National September 11 Memorial using 'meaningful adjacencies' also highlights how social relationships between the dead are just as important as ongoing social relationships between the living and the dead.[87] The Classical quotation on the memorial, 'No day shall erase you from the memory of time' is a translation of a line from Vergil's *Aeneid* (*Nulla dies umquam memori vos eximet aevo*) in which the authorial voice sympathizes with the death of two young warriors, Nisus and Euryalus, who are also lovers. While the quote speaks to the enduring legacy of a text from Classical antiquity, the homosexual relationship of the warriors and the military context that commemorates civilian deaths have stirred controversy.[88]

The cult of the dead is universal yet also unique – how one is commem-orated says as much about the deceased as the one doing the commemo-rating. Ongoing social relationships with the dead also make it an evolving one. Visiting the dead at the site of burial or commemoration, or museum exhibition erases boundaries between the living and the dead, and to survivors of 9/11, the boundaries continue to evolve and elicit various responses. Moving memorials that bring actual remains or memorials to the home or urban centre further extend and erase these boundaries. Disposal and commemoration are becoming the beginning rather than the end of social relationships with the dead.

Classical antiquity informs many of these evolving definitions and rituals and the (self-) representation of the dead. The increase in unique funerals and disposal options illustrates how the living want to be remembered as much as they want to commemorate others and continue to play a role in the lives of survivors. Graveside activities and ritual meals for and among the dead perpetuate a living status for the dead. Allusions to the ritual in funeral decorations are commemorative of the rites but they also perpetuate them when not actually being performed by the living. Successive women who play the role of Big Mama in her simulated kitchen at the Wade Funeral Home and K-Doe's graveside commemoration of her husband's death are part of the tradition that includes the Day of the Dead celebrations and social networking sites, which further remove the periphery of death and allow for ongoing social relationships with the dead.

EPILOGUE

On 2 May 2011, the body of Osama bin Laden was buried in the Arabian Sea from the US aircraft carrier the USS Carl Vinson. To address concerns whether the sea burial conformed to Islamic burial customs, a US Department of Defense official declared that the body had been cleansed and respectfully buried with proper rites. Behind these assurances, one could infer why bin Laden was not buried on land – the sea burial ensured that there would be no grave that could serve as a shrine for his supporters. A memorial will instead commemorate his victims at the site of their deaths.

The cultural history of death ritual is a long one. Greek and Roman funerary and commemorative practices span the Bronze Age to the Christian era, the transition between paganism and Christianity, inhumation and cremation rites, ritualized expressions of grief and commemoration that were subject to legislation. The practices of the elite and non-elite reflect the synchronistic development of varied burial and commemoration rituals rather than a consecutive or monolithic system in antiquity even after the arrival and impact of Christianity in the city of Rome. The cult of the dead from graveside visits for offerings and meals to ancestor shrines in the home reflects the perpetuation of memory and social relationships. These ongoing social interactions between the living and the dead are as paradigmatic as the art and architecture from Classical antiquity.

The nexus between ancients and moderns reveals the prevalence of the theme of the dead as undead and reflects an enduring need for the living to perpetuate the identity and memory of the dead. The dead themselves often participate in the perpetuation of their own identity and former/current roles traditionally through epitaphs but recently through cosmetic surgery for the wake and theme funerals that present funerals as staged events. This ambiguous status of the dead reflects how much the definition of death and burial are negotiable, based on biological, social, and religious constructs that vary among cultures.

The proximity of death and the dead in relation to the living is also negotiable through a changing periphery that is as much figurative as it is topographic. The (sub) urban funerary culture of the Romans demonstrates the evolution and the legacy of memorials and graveside rituals. Cemeteries, roadside memorials and tombs, however, may no longer indicate where someone is buried if cremation remains are stored in the home, a work of art, jewellery or even launched into outer space. Digital death and eco-friendly alternatives to traditional burial and cremation practices are also changing the boundaries between the living and the dead as they also contribute to the growing individualization of rites and commemorative practices, such as moving memorials and tattoos.

Modern funerary rites are in-progress (self-) expressions of grief and memorialisation that are becoming less traditional and in some countries, more political. (Self-) expression in commemoration may not always represent a break with the past as in the case of reusing ancient sarcophagi or monuments or Neoclassical funerary monuments and cremation urns that frame death and commemoration in relation to Classical antiquity. Economic and social factors are also changing family traditions as cremations and individualized ceremonies are replacing traditional inhumation services. The commercialization of Hallowe'en is contributing to the popularity of the Latin American Day of the Dead festivities and celebration items among non-Hispanic populations in North America. As with jazz funerals, death ritual is becoming less sombre and more of a celebration of life.

The funeral industry, cemeteries, and interactions with the dead have become pop culture staples in literature, the cinema and on television, from HBO's *Six Feet Under* to the vampires and zombies that people television series and cinema screens. Dark tourism, whether visits to the tombs of Alexander the Great, Vergil, or Elvis Presley, or museum exhibitions that feature cadavers or funerary monuments, and even the sites of death, reflects an enduring need to preserve the past and to (re) contextualise it in the present. The National September 11 Memorial and Museum at Ground Zero in New York City is a unique site that brings contemporary burials into a museum space as it elicits various responses to the commemoration of 9/11 in a space that marks the site of death, burial, memorial, and museum. The conflation of these roles at a single site is unique and contributes to the ongoing legacy of commemoration and social relationships with the dead.

SOME SUGGESTIONS FOR FURTHER READING

Bodel, John. *Graveyards and Groves: A Study of the Lex Lucerina.*
American Journal of Ancient History 11 (1994).

Brink, Laurie and Deborah Green, eds *Commemorating the Dead: Texts and Artifacts in Context. Studies in Roman, Jewish, and Christian Burials* (Berlin, NY, 2008).

Carroll, Maureen. *Spirits of the Dead: Roman Funerary Commemoration in Western Europe* (Oxford, 2006).

Coarelli, Filippo. *Rome and Environs: An Archaeological Guide.*
Translated by James J. Clauss and Daniel P. Harmon (Berkeley, Los Angeles and London 2007).

Davies, Douglas, J. *A Brief History of Death* (Malden, MA, Oxford, UK, and Victoria, AU, 2005).

Davies, Penelope, J.E. *Death and the Emperor: Roman Imperial Funerary Monuments from Augustus to Marcus Aurelius* (Cambridge, 2000).

Dunbabin, Katherine M.D. *The Roman Banquet: Images of Conviviality* (Cambridge, 2003).

Edwards, Catharine. *Death in Ancient Rome* (New Haven and London, 2007).

Elsner, Jas´. *Imperial Rome and Christian Triumph. The Art of the Roman Empire AD 100–450* (Oxford, 1998).

Erasmo, Mario. *Reading Death in Ancient Rome* (Columbus, OH, 2008).

Flower, Harriet, L. *Ancestor Masks and Aristocratic Power in Roman Culture* (Oxford, 1996).

Garland, Robert. *The Greek Way of Death* (Ithaca, 2001).

Hope, Valerie M. *Roman Death* (London and New York, 2009).

Howarth, Glennys. *Death and Dying: A Sociological Introduction* (Cambridge and Malden, MA, 2008).

Kyle, D.G. *Spectacles of Death in Ancient Rome* (London and New York, 1998).

Jupp, Peter C. *From Dust to Ashes: Cremation and the British Way of Death* (Houndmills and New York, 2006).

Kleiner, Diana E.E. *Roman Imperial Funerary Altars with Portraits* (Rome, 1987).

Koortbojian, Michael. *Myth, Meaning, and Memory on Roman Sarcophagi* (Berkeley and Los Angeles, 1995).

Kurtz, Donna C. and John Boardman. *Greek Burial Customs* (Ithaca, 1971).

Maddrell, Avril and James D. Sidaway (eds). *Deathscapes: Spaces for Death, Dying, Mourning and Remembrance* (Farnham, Surrey, UK and Burlington, VT, 2010).

Morris, Ian. *Burial and Ancient Society: The Rise of the Greek City-State* (Cambridge, 1987).

Panofsky, Erwin. *Tomb Sculpture: Four Lectures on Its Changing Aspects from Ancient Egypt to Bernini* (New York, 1964).

Riggs, Christina. *The Beautiful Burial in Roman Egypt: Art, Identity, and Funerary Religion* (Oxford, 2006).

Roach, Mary. *Stiff: The Curious Lives of Human Cadavers* (New York and London, 2003).

Sourvinou-Inwood, Christiane. *'Reading' Greek Death to the End of the Classical Period* (Oxford, 1995).

Toynbee, J.M.C. *Death and Burial in the Roman World* (Baltimore and London, 1971).

Varner, Eric. *Mutilation and Transformation: Damnatio Memoriae and Roman Imperial Portraiture* (Leiden, 2004).

Vermeule, Emily. *Aspects of Death in Early Greek Art and Poetry* (Berkeley, 1979).

Warpole, Ken. *Last Landscapes: The Architecture of the Cemetery in the West* (London, 2003).

NOTES

Chapter I

1   Georgia Migliuri quoted in Diane Mapes, 'Final Touch: A cosmetic lift for your funeral?' MSNBC.com 9 December 2008.

2   'Seventy percent of the time, people will bring in old photos or say, "I want my mom to look like she did in 1951," says Steve Murillo of Hollywood Forever. 'That's not possible. I'm a mortician, not a magician. But I always tell them, I'll do my best.' Quote cited in Mapes (2008).

3   On the theatricality of displaying the deceased, see Glennys Howarth, *Last Rites: The Work of the Modern Funeral Director* (Amityville, NY, 1996) 5–6: 'In the production of the tragic ritual, funeral directors manipulate mortuary symbols in order to present a *dramatic representation* rather than the *disturbing realities* of death. The salience of the drama is its 'respect' and 'dignity.' The corpse, centrepiece of the drama, is prepared and staged in a manner intended to resemble a peaceful sleeper. Props enhance the spectacle as shiny black limousines crawl ominously through the streets to the cemetery and coffins eventually disappear off stage as the final curtain falls at the close of the performance. Mourners are left to mumble *ad-lib* phrases as they admire floral tributes – the sole remaining symbols of death past.'

4   See Shirley Firth, 'Hindu death and mourning rituals: the impact of geographic mobility' in Jenny Hockey, Jeanne Katz, and Neil Small, eds, *Grief, Mourning, and Death Ritual* (Buckingham and Philadelphia, 2001) 237–246 for an analysis of changes in ritual and gender roles in traditional Hindu death and mourning rituals in Britain.

5   For different anthropological and archaeological approaches to the ancient evidence for funerary and burial rites, see Christiane Sourvinou-Inwood, *'Reading' Greek Death to the End of the Classical Period* (Oxford, 1995) and Ian Morris, *Death-Ritual and Social Structure in Classical Antiquity* (Cambridge, 1992).

6   See Margaret Alexiou, *The Ritual Lament in Greek Tradition* (Lanham, MD 2002) 14 ff. for changes to funeral legislation, especially since the Archaic period in which public rites, especially those practised by women, played a more prominent public role.

7   Cicero discusses Athenian burial laws and customs and the reforms of Solon and Demetrios in relation to Roman funerary practices (*De legibus* 2.25.62–64; 2.26.64–66; 2.27.67–68). Cicero also discusses the funerary laws prescribed by Plato (*Laws* 12.958d–e).

8   See John R. Patterson, 'On the Margins of the City of Rome' in Valerie M. Hope and Eireann Marshall, eds, *Death and Disease in the Ancient City* (London and New York, 2000) 85–103 for the changing boundaries of Rome's *pomerium* and the impact on pollution and burials. Ray Laurence, 'Emperors, Nature, and the City: Rome's Ritual Landscape' in *Accordia Research Papers* 4 (1993) 79–83 discusses the series of shrines farther out from the city, such as Fortuna Muliebris on Via Latina, Terminus on Via Laurentina, and Dea Dia on Via Campana that also marked ritual boundaries from the archaic to the imperial periods.

9   Cicero discusses the religious character of Roman inhumation burials from 2.22.55–69. In the late second and third centuries CE, Paulus in his *Opinions* (1.21.2–5), cites similar laws on burial and mourning (except for details concerning sacrifices).

10   See James Stevens Curl, *The Victorian Celebration of Death* (Stroud, UK, 2000) for a detailed discussion of Victorian funerary rituals, especially after the death of Prince Albert.

11   Clive Seale, *Constructing Death: The Sociology of Dying and Bereavement* (Cambridge, 1998) 34: 'The material end of the body is only roughly congruent with the end of the social self. In extreme old age, or in diseases where mind and personality disintegrate, social death may precede biological death. Ghosts, memories and ancestor worship are examples of the opposite: a social presence outlasting the body.' See also recent analyses of dying in Alan Kellehear (ed.), *The Study of Dying: From Anatomy to Transformation* (Cambridge, 2009) and Douglas Davies, 'The Social Facts of Death' in Glennys Howarth and Peter C. Jupp, eds, *Contemporary Issues in the Sociology of Death, Dying, and Disposal* (Houndmills and New York, 1996) 17–29. For dying in ancient Rome, see Catharine Edwards, *Death in Ancient Rome* (New Haven and London, 2007).

12   See Elizabeth Hallam, Jenny Hockey, and Glennys Howarth, *Beyond the Body: Death and Social Identity* (London and New York, 1999) 'Socialising the Body' 124–141.

13   Glennys Howarth, *Death and Dying: A Sociological Introduction* (Cambridge and Malden, MA, 2008) 'The Dead Body' 185–188.

14   See Sheila Harper, 'The Social Agency of Dead Bodies' *Mortality* 15.4 (2010) 308–322 for a discussion of Alfred Gell's theory of agency on the definition of dead bodies and Valerie M. Hope, 'Contempt and Respect: The treatment of the corpse in ancient Rome' in Hope and Marshall (2000) 104–127 for a detailed discussion of the conception and manipulation of death and the dead in ancient Rome.

15   Antigone's insistence on burying the body of her brother in Sophocles' *Antigone*, while motivated by religious observance, is carried to extremes as a symptom of the *anoia* or lawlessness that visits Thebes and pits her against the decree of Creon.

16 See Paulus *Opinions* 1.21.2.

17 See Hope in Hope and Marshall (2000) 112–125. Rolling Stones guitarist Keith Richards admitted to snorting his father's ashes mixed with cocaine but his manager issued a denial when the public reaction was one of shock and belief, rather than disbelief. The Associate Press reported on Richards' interview with the British magazine NME and his manager's denial 04 April 2007.

18 See Harriet I. Flower, *The Art of Forgetting: Disgrace and Oblivion in Roman Political Culture* (Chapel Hill, 2006) and Eric R. Varner, *Mutilation and Transformation: Damnatio Memoriae and Roman Imperial Portraiture* (Leiden, 2004).

19 See Emily Vermeule, *Aspects of Death in Early Greek Art and Poetry* (Berkeley, 1979) 13.

20 Donna C. Kurtz and John Boardman, *Greek Burial Customs* (Ithaca, 1971) 146.

21 Pliny, *Natural History* 16.40; 16.139 discusses the funereal symbolism of these trees at household doors and graves, but he also remarks that the pine is used in house gardens because they are easy to prune, implying that the location as much as the tree types are necessary for funereal associations. See also Festus-Paulus 56L under the heading *cupressus*. For a detailed discussion of death pollution, see Hugh Lindsay, 'Death-Pollution and Funerals in the City of Rome' in Valerie M. Hope and Eireann Marshall, eds, *Death and Disease in the Ancient City* (London and New York, 2000) 152–173.

22 See John Bodel, 'Dealing with the Dead: Undertakers, executioners and potter's fields in ancient Rome' in Hope and Marshall, eds, (2000) 128–151 for a detailed discussion of the roles played by funeral professionals and the impact and location of the dead to the city of Rome. Bodel also analyzes the derivation and identification of the morbid figure/metaphor of Libitina.

23 Translation of the *lex libitinariae* is from Lindsay (2000) 159. See also John Bodel 'Graveyards and Groves: A Study of the *Lex Lucerina*' *American Journal of Ancient History* 11 (1994) 72–80.

24 See James L. Watson, 'Funeral Specialists in Cantonese Society: Pollution, Performance, and Social Hierarchy' in James L. Watson and Evelyn S. Rawski, eds, *Death Ritual in Late Imperial and Modern China* (Berkeley, 1988) 109–134, Lindsay (2000) 157–160 and Bodel (2000) 135.

25 Hallam, Hockey, and Howarth (1999) 129.

26 The term forensics has funerary origins: although Julius Caesar was assassinated at the entrance of the Curia to Pompey's Theatre, the physician Antistius examined his body 'before the forum' and determined which of the twenty-three stab wounds had proved fatal.

27 See Hallam, Hockey, and Howarth (1999) 131: 'Taking custody, the mortician is aware that for families the body of the deceased is not merely a shell but is vested with memories. As such, it is not an object but a person to whom they retain an emotional attachment.' Evelyn Waugh's satirical novel, *The Loved One: An Anglo-American Tragedy* (1948) parodies the funeral industry and was turned into the 1965 film 'The Loved One' directed by Tony Richardson.

28 'Wife: Man's body cut to fit coffin' *The Associated Press* 3 April 2009.

29 'Illinois grandmother's casket had someone else in it' *The Associated Press* 16 July 2008.

30 On the vast archaeological record of Egyptian burial customs, see most recently Christina Riggs, *The Beautiful Burial in Roman Egypt: Art, Identity, and Funerary Religion*. Oxford Studies in Ancient Culture and Representation (Oxford, 2006).

31 See Derek B. Counts, '*Regum Externorum Consuetudine*: The Nature and Function of Embalming in Rome' *Classical Antiquity* 15 (1996) 189–202.

32 See Christina Riggs, 'Roman Period Mummy Masks from Deir el-Bahri' *The Journal of Egyptian Archaeology* 86 (2000) 121–144.

33 Vicki León, *How to Mellify a Corpse and Other Human Stories of Ancient Science and Superstition* (New York, 2010) 282–285 discusses the use of honey to preserve corpses in antiquity in the context of recent studies that demonstrated its efficacy.

34 See Rodolfo Lanciani, *Pagan and Christian Rome* (New York, 1892) 294–301 for various accounts of the discovery and the preservatives.

35 The article, 'Mummification for a Price' appeared in *The New York Times* 27 June 2000. Cryonics, the preservation of 'deanimated' bodies in containers of liquid nitrogen for future reanimation is controversial and often divides family members, such as the children of baseball legend Ted Williams, on the issue of preservation vs. disposal. See 'Until Cryonics Us Do Part' *The New York Times* 5 July 2010 for disagreements that arise between spouses when one opts for cryonics over traditional burial or cremation.

36 Wakes are popular settings for cinema and television shows such as HBO's *Six Feet Under*. The comedy 'Death at a Funeral' (2010) directed by Neil LaBute reset the British film of the same title directed by Frank Oz (2007) as an African-American-inspired film. At other times, the drama at an actual wake is unexpected. Family members were shocked when an unknown woman interrupted a funeral service in Laurens County, NC, waved a wand around the coffin, opened the lid, placed her hands on the deceased's head and then struck him with the wand. The woman then took flowers from the coffin and threw them at the shocked family members before leaving the service. She was later apprehended and charged with disturbing a funeral and public disorderly conduct. See www.firstcoastnews.com 'Stranger Hits Dead Man at Funeral'.

37 Howarth (1996) 179 discusses the symbolic importance of the placement of flowers in an East End funeral home in London: 'The arrangement of flowers was a source of concern for the funeral director as he tried to ensure that tributes were grouped on and around the coffin according to the donor's relationship with the deceased. Placing a wreath from a relatively unimportant wellwisher in a prime location on the coffin could cause acrimony among the bereaved.'

38 Jose Lambiet, 'Leslie Nielsen's life celebrated at open-casket cocktail party' *Palm Beach Post* 7 December 2010.

39 The article, 'Eternal rest above Marilyn Monroe? Bid on it. Widow selling husband's burial spot on eBay to pay off mortgage.' appeared in *Reuters* 19 August 2009. The winning bid was $4.6 million USD.

NOTES

40 'Dead Man Standing' Foxnews.com 19 August 2008. A video of Medina's embalmed body is on Youtube.com.

41 See 'Velan meurto en motora en Hato Rey' Primerahora.com 27 April 2010 and 'Funeral Home Displays Shooting Victim on Motorcycle For Wake' Jalopnik.com 28 April 2010 for blog comments such as, 'Rigor Mortis? Nah, just ridin' sturdy.' A video of Colón is on Youtube.com.

42 The emphasis of the scene is on the mourner. Focusing on survivors to those pre-planning their funerals is a marketing technique of the modern funeral industry. An advertisement for the Bernstein Funeral Home in Athens, GA includes a photograph of a girl dressed in a white summer dress with arms uplifted and face looking towards the sky that is next to the quote: 'Afterwards, as most of the family turned to walk away, I looked back to find Caroline still standing there peacefully. "Goodbye, grandma," she said smiling. It's a moment I'll cherish for the rest of my life.' The speaker is not identified and there is no indication that the quote is from an actual testimonial. The advertisement highlights the 'emotional' benefit of a planned and professional funeral service to survivors but also to the person pre-planning their funeral who is invited to imagine the grief of family members. Wakes and funerals are part of an industry that develops and markets products and services, and educates professionals in the latest industry developments. The Tan Expo exhibition held in Milan 2010 attracted funeral practitioners from all over the world.

43 For detailed accounts of Greek funerals, see Kurtz and Boardman (Ithaca, 1971) 142–161; Vermeule (1979) 191–21; Hugh Lindsay, 'Eating with the Dead: The Roman Funerary Banquet' in Inge Nielsen and Hanne Sigismund Nielsen, eds, *Meals in a Social Context: Aspects of the Communal Meal in the Hellenistic and Roman World* (Oxford, 1998), 67–69; and Robert Garland, *The Greek Way of Death* (Ithaca, 2001) 21–37.

44 See Peter C. Jupp, *From Dust to Ashes: Cremation and the British Way of Death* (Houndmills and New York, 2006) 39–42.

45 In her article, 'More families bringing funerals home' that appeared on MSNBC.com on 25 September 2007, Joy Jernigan writes, 'It's part of a small but growing movement in the United States to take back death. Led by aging baby boomers, often dealing with the deaths of their parents and facing their own mortality, Americans are slowly relearning what it means to care for their own dead.'

46 Kurtz and Boardman (1971) 144: 'Restricting the *prothesis* to the home discouraged such displays of intense grief and turned a potentially public ceremony into a private one.' For ritual mourning and gender distinctions, see Garland (2001) 29 for the presence of men on Geometric vases holding one hand up to the head in a gesture of lamentation and Karen Stears, 'Death Becomes Her: Gender and Athenian Death Ritual' in *Lament: Studies in the Ancient Mediterranean and Beyond* ed. Ann Suter (Oxford, 2008) 139–155. See Glennys Howarth, 'Grieving in public' in Hockey, Katz, Small, eds, (2001) 247–255 for the growing expressions of grief in public as a result of sudden deaths.

47 Kurtz and Boardman (1971) 144–145: 'Restricting the *ekphora* to the early morning hours and banning the performance of the lament outside the house likewise encouraged a simple family procession, not a sumptuous public cortège.'

48   For detailed accounts of Roman funerals, see J.M.C. Toynbee, *Death and Burial in the Roman World* (Baltimore and London, 1971) 43–61 and Harriet L. Flower, *Ancestor Masks and Aristocratic Power in Roman Culture* (Oxford, 1996) 91–127 and most recently, Valerie M. Hope, *Roman Death* (London and New York, 2009).

49   See Hope (2009) 73 and Toynbee (1971) 44–45. A relief of a funeral procession from Amiternum, Italy that dates to the mid-first century BCE shows the deceased reclining on a funeral couch that is carried by numerous attendants, mourners and musicians.

50   For these details of traditional Sikh funerals and variations not mentioned above (such as the rites for great-great grandfathers and newborn boys) and how they were adapted in Britain, see: Sewa Singh Kalsi, 'Change and Continuity in the Funeral Rituals of Sikhs in Britain' in Howarth and Jupp, eds, (1996) 30–43.

51   See Erasmo (2008) for allusions to death ritual and literary descriptions of those rituals in Latin literature, in particular the cremation of Pallas in Vergil's *Aeneid* and of Pompey in Lucan's *Bellum Civile*.

52   See Christine Perkell, 'Reading the Laments of *Iliad* 24' in Sutter, ed. (2008) 93–117.

53   See Loring M. Danforth, *The Death Rituals of Rural Greece* (Princeton, 1982) 74: 'Women singing laments are communicating in a symbolic language and in the context of a public performance.' Alexiou (2002) describes the 'allusive method' of lamentation, 185: 'Part of the artistic economy in the language of folk tradition is the allusive method, by which a fact or an idea is expressed indirectly but concretely, through symbols. In the lament, it has a further ritual significance, since the mourner may deliberately avoid explicit reference to death, addressing the dead in a series of striking images and elaborating her theme through metaphors and similes. Since this is a universal characteristic of the ritual lament, and not peculiar to Greek, continuity must be sought in specific terms of form and content rather than in the general survival of the practice.' See also Patrick Leigh Fermor, *Mani: Travels in the Southern Peloponnese* (New York, 1958).

54   In relation to the depiction of myth on Roman sarcophagi, Michael Koortbojian, *Myth, Meaning, and Memory on Roman Sarcophagi* (Berkeley, Los Angeles, London, 1995) 2, writes: 'The correspondence between the dead and the imagery with which they were celebrated was seldom neat, and the analogy between the two rarely simple.'

55   See Elizabeth L. Johnson, 'Grieving for the Dead, Grieving for the Living: Funeral Laments of Hakka Women' in Watson and Rawski, eds, (1988) 135–163 for an analysis of Chinese funeral lamentations as shared expressions of self. Johnson cites this Lower Yangtze proverb, from Ying-shih Yü: 'We use the occasions of other people's funerals to release personal sorrows.'

56   The lament is cited and translated by Danforth (1982) 80–81.

57   Danforth (1982) 83: 'The metaphor of death as marriage is ultimately an attempt to mediate the opposition between life and death. It attempts to do this by establishing marriage as a mediating term and then asserting that death is marriage, that death is not what it really is, a polar term in the opposition

between life and death, but that it is the mediating term. The metaphor of death as marriage 'moves' death from the opposite of life to the mediator between life and death, from the antithesis of life to a synthesis of life and death.'

58 Lamentation from Tsakonia cited by Alexiou (2002) 122.

59 See Alexiou (2002) 120–128 for modern examples of the reciprocity between wedding and funeral lamentations and Danforth (2002) 71–95, in particular 86–87 for the citation of a wedding hymn ('Now I have set out. Now I am about to depart/ from my home and from my dear brothers and sisters./ Everyone is driving me away; everyone is telling me to leave.'), that bears a striking metrical and structural similarity to a funeral lament ('Now I have set out. Now I am about to depart/ from the black and cob-webbed earth').

60 See Lanciani (1892) 301–305 who gives a first-hand narrative of the discovery.

61 The article, 'Ghost brides are murdered to give dead bachelors a wife in the afterlife' appeared on www.timesonline.co.uk 26 January 2007.

62 See Flower (1996) 32–59 'Defining the *Imagines*' and 185–222 'Ancestors at Home: *Imagines* in the Atrium.'

63 The mask is on display in the Medici Museum in the Palazzo Medici-Riccardi, Florence. See also the collection of death masks in the Laurence Hutton Life and Death Mask Collection in the Firestone Library, Princeton University.

64 Maureen Carroll, *Spirits of the Dead: Roman Funerary Commemoration in Western Europe* (Oxford, 2006) 38–39 describes the discovery of two *imagines* moulds found in graves, one of a ten-year-old girl (Claudia Victoria) in Lyon and the other with an unidentified skeleton in Rome.

65 For discussions on the theatricality of Roman funerals, see John Bodel, 'Death on Display: Looking at Roman Funerals' in B. Bergmann and C. Kondoleon (eds), *The Art of Ancient Spectacle* (New Haven, 1999) 258–81; Geoffrey S. Sumi, 'Impersonating the Dead: Mimes at Roman Funerals' *AJP* 123 (2002) 559–585; and 'A Cast of Corpses' in Erasmo (2008) 61–74.

66 See Flower (1996) 128–158 and Donovan J. Ochs, *Consolatory Rhetoric: Grief, Symbol, and Ritual in the Greco-Roman Era* (Columbia, SC, 1993) 104–117.

67 The translation of Polybius 6.53.1–10 is from Erasmo (2008) 65.

68 Suetonius, *Life of Vespasian* 19.2. See Erasmo (2008) 223 for further ancient evidence for the theatricality of Roman funerals.

69 On the parallels between funeral and triumphal processions, see Flower (1996) 107–109.

70 See Geoffrey S. Sumi, *Ceremony and Power: Performing Politics in Rome between the Republic and Principate* (Ann Arbor, 2005) 100–112 for his analysis of the historical sources and theatrical elements of Caesar's funeral and Erasmo (2008) 35–40.

71 On the role of effigies in Imperial funerals, see Javier Arce, 'Roman Imperial Funerals in Effigie' in B. Ewald and C. Norena, (eds), *The Emperor and Rome. Space, Representation and Ritual. Yale Classical Studies* 35 (2010) 309–24.

72 See Arce (2010) 313–315, Sumi (2005) 108–109 and Erasmo (2008) 69–72.

73 See Toynbee (1971) 59 for a discussion of Herodian's description of the ceremony.

74 On the features and symbolic value of funeral pyres, see Eve D'Ambra, 'The Imperial Funerary Pyre as Work of Ephemeral Architecture' in Ewald and Norena (2010) 289–308.

75 Laderman (2003) 208: 'Communities with no access to the real body in Mount Vernon found popular ways to conjure the tangible presence of the dead American hero in order to make those ceremonies more meaningful and fulfilling expressions of personal loss and collective sorrow.'

76 See Howarth (1996) 181–185 for a discussion of walking and timing the cortège.

77 At times, the dead are taken on unexpected trips: according to *The Associated Press* 12 March 2010 'NYC Funeral Home Van Towed With Body Inside,' a funeral minivan parked outside of a New York funeral home was towed with a body inside taking the deceased to a tow pound before arriving at the airport.

78 Equally notable was the funeral procession of the Sex Pistols' Malcolm McLaren. His black coffin that bore the words, 'Too fast to live, too young to die' was conveyed in a horse-drawn carriage to Highgate Cemetery, London accompanied by a double-decker bus with McLaren's slogan 'Cash from Chaos' that blasted Sid Vicious' version of 'My Way.' See 'Punk Pioneer Malcolm McLaren Gets London Send-Off' *The Associated Press* 22 April 2010.

79 Antoinette K-Doe's obituary appeared in *The New York Times* 28 February 2009 and included a picture of her husband's effigy. A video of her funeral is posted on Youtube.com.

Chapter II

1 *Reuters* 23 April 2010 'Search for traces of 9/11 victims continues' is the source for quotes and statistics.

2 Diane Horning whose son Matthew was killed advocates searching for remains and is frustrated at the slow pace: 'It's a little too late, but it's important because we need to respect those who are killed,' she said. Instead of proactively searching, the city waited as excavation progressed to uncover remains, she said. 'To have neglected it for so long, despite everybody begging them, shows their great callousness and disrespect for the dead,' she said.

3 See Anne Eyre, 'Post-Disaster Rituals' in Hockey, Katz, and Small (eds), 256–266 for emotional and ritual responses to disasters, in particular, the potential for survivors to attend multiple funerals and commemorations, both public and private.

4 Statistic according to Michael J. Weiss, 'Dead But Not Necessarily Buried,' *American Demographics* 23.4 (2001) 40.

5 See Jupp (2006) 193: 'Cremation has now become the choice of over 70% of people in Britain for their funerals. Its development has been a response to and a reflection of contemporary culture, both at personal and at social levels. It relates to at least five processes in our society, of municipalisation and the growing role of the state, commercialisation, consumerisation, individualisation and secularisation. Once cremation became established as an alternative to burial, its major effect was to offer families a choice.'

6　Laderman (2003) discusses the impact of AIDS and OSHA mandates on the funeral industry for the embalming of AIDS victims that contributed to the rise in cremations: 140–144, 198–200. The initial responses of funeral directors mirrored the initial fears and prejudices of the general public, 143: 'In addition to initiating these operational changes, many funeral directors began to exhibit an entirely new attitude toward the dead and community responsibility in the early years of the epidemic. Perhaps for the first time in the history of American funeral directing, some morticians refused to work on bodies – often young, horribly disfigured bodies that spoke of inexpressible human suffering. Individuals suspected or known to have died of AIDS were singled out by many within the industry as a potentially harmful source of the deadly contagion and, coupled with the common associations between the disease and homosexuality, social contamination.'

7　The growing use of so-called 'double-decker' burials in the City of London Cemetery has sparked debate on 'second-hand' burial plots and memorials. See 'A Grave Crisis: Share a Lot with a Stranger?' *The Associated Press* 28 October 2009.

8　For statistics and testimonials, see 'Indigent Burials are on the Rise' *The New York Times* 11 October 2009.

9　Mary Roach, *Stiff: The Curious Lives of Human Cadavers* (New York and London, 2003), Chapter I1 'Out of the Fire, Into the Compost Bin' 251–277, explores alternatives to traditional furnace cremations: 'reductive cremations' also known as 'tissue digestion' and 'water reduction' that uses water and lye to reduce animal and human tissue and the movement supporting organic composting of human remains in Sweden. More recently, a process called resomation that involves cremating the body at a lower temperature and using high pressure and chemicals to emulsify the body is being seen as an eco-friendly alternative to traditional cremation. See Bill Briggs 'When you're dying for a lower carbon footprint' MSNBC.com 18 January 2010.

10　Mary Bradbury, 'Forget me not: memorialization in cemeteries and crematoria' in Hockey, Katz, and Small, eds, (2001) 219.

11　See Edward Wong, 'Coffins, Urns and Webcast Funerals' in the *New York Times* 5 October 2000: 10 and Laderman (2003) 210 for the role of the Cremation-Cam to dispel common fears surrounding cremations.

12　The series of photographs that show Kraus in the various stages of performing a cremation are at www.pointssouth.net/archives/photo/cremation.

13　The original crematorium in Milan made the allusion to ancient Roman funerary ritual more explicit: it was Neoclassical in style in the shape of a sarcophagus with an urn on top that burned a flame of gas. See James Stevens Curl, *Death and Architecture* (Stroud, UK, 2002) that is a new and revised edition of *A Celebration of Death* (London, 1980, revised 1993): 299–314 for a detailed study of the development of cremation and crematoria.

14　See Jupp (2006) 90–93 and H.J. Grainger, *Death Redesigned: British Crematoria: History, Architecture and Landscape* (Reading, 2005) for detailed discussions of the role played by Golders Green Crematorium on the design and planning of crematoria in Britain.

15　See Erasmo (2008) 75–107.

16   Morris (1992) 110–118 reviews the material evidence of grave goods as a means to distinguish inhumation and cremation burials.

17   See Penelope J.E.Davies, *Death and the Emperor: Roman Imperial Funerary Monuments from Augustus to Marcus Aurelius* (Cambridge, 2000) for imperial *ustrina* complexes.

18   Pliny, *Natural History* 11.150 '*(oculos) in rogo patefacere*'. See Toynbee (1971) 50.

19   Cicero, *De legibus* 2.22.55.

20   Varro is quoted by Servius, *ad Aen.* 6.216.

21   See J.I. McKinley, 'Cremations: expectations, methodologies and realities' in C.A. Roberts, F. Lee, and J. Birtliff (eds), *Burial Archaeology. Current Research, Methods and Development* BAR British Series 211 (1989), 65–76 who estimates a burning time of 7 to 8 hours under ideal conditions and David Noy, 'Half-Burnt On An Emergency Pyre: Roman Cremations Which Went Wrong' *Greece and Rome* 47 (2000): 186–196.

22   Pliny, *Natural History* 7.186.

23   See Plutarch, *Brutus* 20. Cicero, *Pro Milone* 3 and *Philippics* 2.91 claims that P. Clodius' and Caesar's bodies were only half-cremated but this may be a political attack against those in charge of the funerals. See Noy (2000) 191 for an analysis of Cicero's political bias.

24   The recent discovery of a rare American Indian cremation pit on Ossabaw Island, Georgia reveals the variety of burial rituals that cremations were rare: on the nearby island of St. Catherines, only 9 out of about 900 graves contained cremated remains. For details of the discovery and Native American burials on the coastal islands of Georgia, see 'American Indian cremation pit found' *The Associated Press* 19 December 2008.

25   Information and citations taken from the article 'Funeral Pyre Verdict' by The Natural Death Centre on 11 February 2010: www.naturaldeath.org.uk.

26   In the USA, other than the Buddhist Temple in Red Feather Lakes, CO, the town of Crestone, CO is the only community that allows open-air cremations. The ceremonies are non-denominational. For spiritual elements of the ceremony, see "One with the sky" Funeral Pyres in Co. Town' *The Associated Press* 31 January 2011.

27   See Louis-Vincent Thomas, *La Mort Africaine: Idéologie funéraire en Afrique Noire* (Paris, 1982).

28   Information as posted on eBay.com 2 November 2011. In addition to urns for human remains, are numerous choices for pet urns.

29   Information as posted on 2 November 2011.

30   See Toynbee (1971), 14–16 for a discussion of the variety and dating of Etruscan cinerary containers.

31   The Vienna Kunsthistoriches Museum, for example, contains an alabaster chest with a reclining woman on the lid with a scene depicting the Rape of Helen on the chest.

32   See, for example, the first century CE funeral monument of the freedman P. Nonius Zethus and his family in the Museo Chiaramonti in the Vatican Museums (Section X, no. 26) that is in the shape of a square block with reliefs of a donkey turning a mill and bakery equipment on the front and conical

openings on top that contained cinerary remains. A breadbasket-shaped marble urn at the Metropolitan Museum of Art of New York (Acc. no 37.129) may be similar to the one used to contain the ashes of the wife of Eurysaces whose tomb, next to the Porta Maggiore, Rome, is in the shape of a bread oven with scenes of bread making in sculptural reliefs. On the funeral monuments of freedmen, see Lauren Hackworth Petersen, *The Freedman in Roman Art and Art History* (Cambridge, 2006).

33 See Toynbee (1971), 14–15.

34 See Chapter IV for representations of the dead in dining contexts.

35 *Sculpture in Stone* (MFA) no. 384. This sarcophagus was found with another sarcophagus no. 383 that also depicts a sleeping couple facing each other.

36 For the mythological portraiture of women including in funereal contexts, see Eve D'Ambra 'The Calculus of Venus: Nude Portraits of Roman Matrons.' in Natalie Boymel Kampen, ed., *Sexuality in Ancient Art: Near East, Egypt, Greece, and Italy* (Cambridge, 1996) 219–32; Diana E.E. Kleiner 'Second-Century Mythological Portraiture: Mars and Venus' *Latomus* 40 (1981) 512–44; and Erasmo (2008) 178–80. See Toynbee (1971) 281 for the unique sarcophagus from Simpelveld that contains carved along the inside of the chest the effigy of a woman reclining on a couch within a furnished room.

37 Select examples of recumbent effigies from churches in Rome: the pavement tomb of Fra' Angelico (d. 1455) in S. Maria sopra Minerva made from his death mask; well-worn marble pavement tombs in S. Maria in Aracoeli and S. Maria del Popolo whose current two-dimensionality gives them the resemblance of face cards from a deck of cards; wall tombs of Piccolomini Popes Pius II (d. 1464) and Pius III (d. 1503) placed high above doorways in the nave of S. Andrea della Valle; the stacked effigies of Cardinal Giovanni Michiel (d. 1503) and his nephew Bishop Antonio Orso (d. 1511) in S. Marcello al Corso sculpted by Jacopo Sansovino that gives the impression of a bunk bed supported by a pile of books that alludes to the Cardinal's library collection.

38 See Zahra Newby, 'Art at the crossroads? Themes and styles in Severan art' in Simon Swain, Stephen Harrison, and Jas' Elsner (eds) *Severan Culture* (Cambridge, 2007) 201–249 and Toynbee (1971) 270–277.

39 For an analysis of the myth and its representation on sarcophagi, see Michael Koortbojian, *Myth, Meaning, and Memory on Roman Sarcophagi* (Berkeley and Los Angeles, 1995) 63–99.

40 For examples of neo-Attic sarcophagi, see the Sarcophagi with the Battle before the Trojan ships and Amazonomachy, each with recumbent couple on lid, in the Thessaloniki Archaeological Museum that date to the second quarter of the third century CE.

41 See Jas' Elsner, *Imperial Rome and Christian Triumph. The Art of the Roman Empire AD 100–450* (Oxford, 1998) for the emergence and significance of Christian iconography.

42 For detailed examination, see D. Rezza, *Un Neofita in Paradiso: il Sarcophago di Giunio Basso* (Rome, 2010) and Elizabeth Struthers Malbon, *The Iconography of the Sarcophagus of Junius Bassus* (Princeton, 1990). See also the 'Dogmatic Sarcophagus' also found in St. Peter's Necropolis.

43 On the identity of Constantine's daughter Constantia who is sometimes

identified as Constantina, see F. Chausson, *Stemmata Aurea. Constantin, Justine, Théodose Revendications Généalogiques et Idéologie Impériale au IV s. Ap. J.C.* Centro Ricerche e Documentazione sull' Antichità Classica Monografie 26 (Rome, 2007).

44 For the use of porphyry for Imperial sarcophagi, compare the Neoclassical tomb of Napoleon, Eglise du Dome, Hôtel des Invalides, Paris that consists of a red porphyry tub on a green granite base with a scroll lid and circular handles carved on the sides. The design of the tomb may have been influenced by the display of these Imperial sarcophagi in the Vatican Museums that were already in place when Napoleon arrived in Rome.

45 See Filippo Coarelli, *Rome and Environs: An Archaeological Guide* Translated by James J. Clauss and Daniel P. Harmon (Berkeley, Los Angeles and London, 2007) 419.

46 The grape harvest scene is also depicted on an unidentified S. Lorenzo sarcophagus in narthex with putti, grapevines, and various animals.

47 See Rodolfo Lanciani, *The Destruction of Ancient Rome* (London and New York, 1901) 116–117 for the removal of martyr bones from catacombs: 'The relics of martyrs were, as a rule, deposited in basins and bath-tubs of rare marble [. . .] and sarcophagi.'

48 For details of the fate and restoration of the sarcophagus, see Lanciani (1893) 196–198.

49 See Julian Gardner, 'Arnolfo di Cambio and Roman Tomb Design' *The Burlington Magazine* 115 (1973) 420–439 for the elements of medieval tomb designs. The funeral monument of Cardinal Aquasparta in S. Maria in Aracoeli contains similar elements but has a reclining effigy rather than a spoliated sarcophagus.

50 Lanciani (1892)146–147.

51 Airlines and shipping companies issue their own guidelines concerning acceptable containers and disclosures. Some of the issues and challenges are discussed in 'Dealing with an unexpected death on the road' Christopher Elliot for MSNBC.com 2 September 2008. The Tri-State Crematory scandal in 2002 in which owner Ray Brent Marsh was charged with leaving 339 bodies uncremated or unburied in hearses and other vehicles all over the crematorium property was shocking for the magnitude of corpse abuse.

52 'Can I see some ID? Dead man kept off plane.' *Reuters* 6 April 2010. The unauthorized shipment of a cadaver is the subject of the cult film 'Route 66' in which Satan follows a pair of friends who are illegally driving with a corpse from Thunder Bay, Ontario to New Orleans, LA.

53 'Corpse in airport was dead 12 hours, police say.' *The Associated Press* 9 April 2010.

54 Garland (2001) 39 for the evidence of Artemidoros (5.82 T) that the dead was believed to be present at the *perideipnon* as host.

55 In Rome, burials for Protestants and children were historically held at night.

56 Akiro Kirosawa's 'Ikiru' (1952) centres on a funeral meal in which guests recount details surrounding the deceased's life and death. In 'The Big Chill' (1983) directed by Lawrence Kasdan, baby boomers gather for a weekend following the funeral of a friend and assess the successes and failures of their own lives.

57 See Danforth (1982) 48 for a description and photographs of women performing Greek Orthodox burial rites in rural Greece (Potamia).

58 See Bradbury (2001) 221 and *Representations of Death: A Social Psychological Perspective* (London and New York, 1999) 132–135 for the social and psychological implications of secondary burials including the scattering of ashes.

59 Mark Rowe 'Grave Changes: Scattering Ashes in Contemporary Japan' *Japanese Journal of Religious Studies* 30 (2003) 85–118 discusses the effects of the growing popularity of ash scattering on family traditions in Japan.

60 See Hope (2009) 60–61 for ancient fears of a death at sea without proper burial rites.

61 In the USA, the Environmental Protection Agency (EPA) regulates the scattering of remains at sea and along coastlines but state and local ordinances may also apply. In San Francisco, the Neptune Society scatters remains at sea near the Golden Gate Bridge aboard their ship the 'Naiad'.

62 Memorial Spaceflights are offered by Celestis, Inc. who describe their services on their website (www.celestis.com) 'Leaving Earth to touch the cosmos is an experience few have ever known, but many have often dreamed of. Celestis makes it possible to honor the dream and memory of your departed loved one by launching a symbolic portion of cremated remains into Earth orbit, onto the lunar surface or into deep space. Missions into space that return the cremated remains to Earth are also available.'

63 The company HolySmoke LLC describes it services: 'We offer a way to honor your deceased loved one by giving or sharing with him or her one more round of clay targets, one last bird hunt, or one last stalk hunt' (www.my holysmoke.com). On the website, a friend is quoted as saying, 'You know I've thought about this for some time and I want to be cremated. Then I want my ashes put into some turkey shotgun shells and have someone who knows how to turkey hunt use the shotgun shells with my ashes to shoot a turkey. That way I will rest in peace knowing that the last thing that one turkey will see is me, screaming at him at about 900 feet per second.'

64 According to the website advertisement for LifeGem Memorial Diamonds (www.lifegem.com) 'Your LifeGem memorial will provide a lasting memory that endures just as a diamond does. Forever.' Eternalreefs.com describes the participation of family members in creating a coral reef from cremated remains: 'Families and friends are invited and encouraged to participate in the creation of their loved one's memorial reef. From placing your handprint in the damp concrete during the casting, making a rubbing of the bronze plaque during the viewing ceremony, or placing a flag on your loved one's memorial reef during our military honors ceremony, all Eternal Reefs' activities provide peace of mind for everyone involved.'

Chapter III

1 Cyril Wecht, 'Haiti's Grisly Problem' *The Daily Beast* 19 January 2010.
2 See Damien Cave, 'As Haitians Flee, the Dead Go Uncounted' *The New York Times 19 January 2010.*
3 See Erasmo (2008) 7.

4 'Remains of Hitler Deputy, Hess, Removed in Germany' *The New York Times* 22 July 2011.
5 For the semiotic interpretation of tombs, see Sourvinou-Inwood (1995) 110 ff. and S.C. Humphreys, 'Family Tombs and Tomb Cult in Ancient Athens: Tradition or Traditionalism?' *Journal of Roman Studies* 100 (1980) 102–104.
6 Varro, *De lingua latina* 6.49.
7 Ken Warpole, *Last Landscapes: The Architecture of the Cemetery in the West* (London, 2003) 20 states the dynamic succinctly: 'The influence of the dead on landscape form and experience can be highly charged, even pervasive.'
8 *Inscriptiones Graecae (IG)* ii2 14, 4–6.
9 Perugini's wife Uga de Plaisan Perugini (1917–2004) is also buried beneath the cube. The transformative power of graves on the landscape was also exhibited by Perugini in his design for the Monument of the Fosse Ardeatine, Rome that marks the location where German occupation forces imprisoned 335 civilians and set on fire the building that housed the remnants of the Emperor Caligula's ships found at Nemi.
10 Maurice Bloch, *Placing the Dead: Tombs, Ancestral Villages, and Kinship Organization in Madagascar* (New York, 1971) explores the spatial relationships between the living and the dead.
11 'Burglars steal grandmother's ashes' *The Atlanta Journal Constitution* 14 August 2010.
12 On the expulsion of the dead in Paris, See Armando Petrucci, *Writing the Dead. Death and Writing Strategies in the Western Tradition*. Translated by Michael Sullivan (Stanford, 1998) 105ff.
13 For a detailed history of the cemetery, in particular the role of Neoclassicism, see Richard A. Etlin, *The Architecture of Death: The Transformation of the Cemetery in Eighteenth-Century Paris* (Cambridge, MA and London, 1984) 310–331 for architect Alexandre-Théodore Brongniart's proposed designs that included Neoclassical elements such as a pyramid inspired by the Pyramid of Gaius Cestius at the Protestant Cemetery, Rome and Curl (2002) 154–167 for tomb designs: 'The Neoclassical language of the tombs was fashionable and evocative and suggested the respectability of the antique.' 156–157.
14 Other cemeteries, like Oakland Cemetery, Atlanta welcome visitors to stroll among the landscaped historic tombs. Youtube.com contains the commercials of cemeteries such as Sewickley Cemetery in Sewickley, PA, which invites viewers to visit the landscaped grounds.
15 See Humphreys (1980) 97 for a discussion of the anxieties in Paris over the relocations and the recognition of property rights for the dead: 'Thus, in a very short space of time, during the first half of the nineteenth century, the family cult of the tomb grew from being almost unknown in the modern world and largely disregarded in books on antiquity to become a massive phenomenon of contemporary life and a self-evident fact of history and ethnography.'
16 For natural burial as an extension of the modern eco-conscious culture, see Andy Clayden, Trish Green, Jenny Hockey and Mark Powell, 'From Cabbages to Cadavers: Natural Burial Down on the Farm' in Avril Maddrell and James D. Sidaway, eds *Deathscapes: Spaces for Death, Dying, Mourning and Remembrance* (Farnham, Surrey and Burlington, VT, 2010) 119–138 and

NOTES

Douglas J. Davies, *A Brief History of Death* (Malden, MA, Oxford, UK, and Victoria, AU, 2005) 68–88 and Warpole (2003) 20–21.

17 *Carmina Latina Epigraphica* (*CE*), ed. F. Buecheler, A. Riese, and E. Lommatzsch (Leipzig, 1964) 1184, lines 12–18:

> o mihi si superi vellent praestare roganti
> ut tuo de tumulo flos ego cerna novum
> crescere vel viridi ramo vel flore amaranti
> vel roseo vel purpureo violaeque nitore,
> ut qui praeteriens gressu tardante viator
> viderit hos flores, titulum legat et sibi dicat
> 'hoc flos est corpus Flaviae Nicopolis'.

The marble grave marker that was found in Rome at the Porta Salaria or on Via Nomentana no longer survives. For this and other epitaphs that express the theme of flowers growing from the body of the deceased, see Richmond Lattimore, *Themes in Greek and Latin Epitaphs* (Urbana, 1962) 135–136.

18 The sarcophagus of Scipio Barbatus, an eclectic design of Doric and Italic elements, is currently displayed in the Museo Pio-Clementino of the Vatican Museums. See Erasmo (2008) 165–171 for a discussion of the sarcophagus and its placement in the museum. Imitations are ubiquitous in European and American cemeteries. In Rome, the Protestant Cemetery contains nine copies for men and women. Other notable examples in Rome include the tomb of Capitano Scipione Federici in Campo Verano Cemetery that commemorates his military service (and eponymic connection to Scipio Barbatus) and the funerary monument of Vincenzo Valentini in the Basilica of Ss. Apostoli.

19 Of the 328 bodies recovered, 209 were returned to Halifax but the other 119 that were badly damaged or deteriorated were buried at sea. In ceremonies from 12 May to 12 June 1912, 150 bodies were buried in Halifax: 19 in the Mount Olivet Cemetery, 10 in the Baron de Hirsch Jewish Cemetery and 121 in the Fairview Lawn Cemetery.

20 The Poem 'In Flanders Fields', written by John McCrae begins, 'In Flanders fields the poppies blow/ Between the crosses, row on row,/ That mark our place [...]' The symmetry of the rows of burial markers in Arlington Cemetery evoke a crop growing amidst the rolling landscaped hills.

21 On the legacy of epitaphs, see Mario Erasmo 'Epitaphs' in Clifton D. Bryant and Dennis L. Peck (eds) *The Encyclopedia of Death and the Human Experience* (Thousand Oaks, CA, 2009) 412–414.

22 For burial practices in the Kerameikos cemetery, see Morris (1992) 111. For Greek funerary monuments, in general, see Percy Gardner, *Sculptured Tombs of Hellas* (Washington, D.C. 1973); Gisela M.A. Richter, *Archaic Gravestones of Attica* (London, 1961); Karen Stears, 'The Times Are A' Changing: Developments in Fifth-Century Funerary Sculpture' in G. J. Oliver, ed., *The Epigraphy of Death: Studies in the History and Society of Greece and Rome* (Liverpool, 2000) 25–58; G.J. Oliver, 'Athenian Funerary Monuments: Style, Grandeur, and Cost' in Oliver, ed. (2000) 59–80; Humphreys (1980) 96–126.

23 See Humphreys (1980) 101–105.

24 See John Boardman, 'Painted Funerary Plaques and Some Remarks on *Prothesis*' *The Annual of the British School at Athens* (50) 1955: 51–66.

159

25 See Boardman (1955) 57.

26 For the development of boot hills and tombstones as evidence of a town's wealth and culture, see Annette Stott, *Pioneer Cemeteries: Sculpture Gardens of the Old West* (Lincoln, NE, and London, 2008) 1–57.

27 See Davies (2000) for Augustus' Mausoleum complex, Hadrian's mausoleum and the imperial burial complexes including those of Trajan, Antoninus Pius and Marcus Aurelius.

28 See Andrew Wallace-Hadrill, 'Housing the Dead: The Tomb as House in Roman Italy' in Brink and Green (2008) 54–56 for the Tomb of the Volumnii and family identity in Etruscan tombs.

29 *Etruscan Places* (1932) 73.

30 See Morris (1992) 31–69 for cremation and humation in the Roman empire and interment within the city of Rome. The gens Valerii was granted an exemption from the law forbidding cremation within the pomerium of the city but they chose instead to hold symbolic cremations.

31 For later intramural burials at Rome, see R. Meneghini and R. Santangeli Valenziani, 'Intra-mural burials at Rome between the fifth and seventh centuries AD' in John Pearce, Martin Millett and Manuela Struck (eds) *Burial, Society and Context in the Roman World* (Oxford, 2000) 263–269.

32 For the variety of tomb styles and sizes, see Hope (2009) 171–177, Carroll (2006) 86–125, and Henner von Hesberg, *Römische Grabbauten* (Darmstadt, 1992). John Bodel, 'From Columbaria to Catacombs: Collective Burial in Pagan and Christian Rome' in Laurie Brink and Deborah Green (eds) *Commemorating the Dead: Texts and Artifacts in Context. Studies of Roman, Jewish and Christian Burials* (Berlin, NY 2008) 177–242 examines evidence for collective burial, in particular the evidence for 'Christian catacombs' that were preceded by subterranean pagan burials.

33 For the burial of the poor, see Carroll (2006), 'Anonymity, Violation, and Memory Loss' 59–85; D.G. Kyle, *Spectacles of Death in Ancient Rome* (London and New York, 1998) 163–169; Bodel (1994) 38–54 and 81–83 for the burial of the poor in public pits on the Esquiline and Viminal Hills; and Toynbee (1971) 101–103.

34 The head of the main figure is ancient but not original to the sculpture but was rather added during a seventeenth century restoration. See Flower (1996) for the connection between portraits, imagines, and the elite.

35 For the display of images and portraits on funerary monuments, see Hope (2009) 164–165, Carroll (2006) 37, Michael Koortbojian, '*In commemorationem mortuorum*: text and image along the "streets of tombs"' in Jas' Elsner (ed) *Art and Text in Roman Culture* (Cambridge, 1996) 210–233 and Diana E.E. Kleiner, *Roman Imperial Funerary Altars with Portraits* (Rome, 1987).

36 Some epitaphs make the eternal bond between couples explicit. See Richmond Lattimore, *Themes in Greek and Latin Epitaphs* (Urbana, IL, 1962) 58 for the reunion of couples in death.

37 For modern portraits of the dead, see Halla Beloff 'Immortality Work: Photographs as *Memento Mori*' in Mitchell (2007) 179–192 and Douglas J. Davies (2005) 101–105 'Portraying the Dead'. Alexis Madrigal, 'Lasers for the

Dead: A Story About Gravestone Technology' *The Atlantic* 28 July 2011
discusses the growing popularity of photoelectric portraits on black granite
gravestones. For examples of portrait etchings on grave monuments, see
theperfectmemorial.com

38 See Erasmo (2008) 3–5 for a discussion of Statius, *Silvae* 5.3.

39 See Hope (2009) 151–166, Laurence (1999) 156–161, J. Bodel, 'Monumental
villas and the villa monuments' *Journal of Roman Archaeology* 10 (1997)
5–35, in particular pages 20–26, Koortbojian (1996) 210–233, and H. von
Hesberg, *Monumenta: I Sepolcri Romani e la loro Architettura* (Milan, 1994)
29–67 for the features and cultural significance of roadside tombs.

40 In a recent court ruling, the creation of a public memorial is part of the
punishment given to a teenager by a juvenile court judge in Clayton County,
Georgia for her role in the death of a toddler. The judge ordered the teenager
to make a memorial to be set up in a public place with the participation of
the toddler's parents to best capture the toddler's personality. For details of
the sentence, see Tammy Joyner, 'Teen tied to day care death ordered to create
a memorial to dead toddler' *The Atlanta Journal-Constitution* 2 August 2011.

41 See Tacitus, *Annals* 2.32.2. Elsewhere, Tacitus mentions that slaves were crucified in special area of Rome: *Annals* 15.60.1. In the Widow of Ephesus episode
in Petronius' *Satyricon* (111–113), the setting of the story in a roadside
hypogeum for 'burial in the Greek manner' is essential to the story of how a
grieving widow was seduced by a guard watching over the crucified bodies of
criminals. The episode shares many narrative features of the Easter Story. See
Erasmo (2008) 23– 27 for a discussion of the Widow's symbolic entomb-
ment.

42 In Catullus' satiric attack against a certain Rufa in Poem 59, he accuses her
of stealing food left at cemeteries. See Hope (2009) 155–156 for the pleas-
ures and dangers of tomb-lined roads.

43 Ray Laurence, *The Roads of Roman Italy: Mobility and Cultural Change*
(London and New York, 1999) 157.

44 For the example of the Tomb of Eurysaces to this dynamic, see Lauren
Hackworth Petersen, 'The Baker, His Tomb, His Wife, and Her Breadbasket: The Monument of Eurysaces in Rome' *The Art Bulletin* 85.2 (2003)
230–257.

45 Coarelli (2007) 366 as observed in relation to the tombs along the Via Appia
Antica.

46 See Penelope J.E. Davies, 'Living to Living, Living to Dead: Communication
and Political Rivalry in Roman Tomb Design' in Maddrell and Sidaway (2010)
225–241 and her forthcoming *Art and Persuasion in Republican Rome*
(Cambridge).

47 See Patterson in Hope and Marshall (2000) 97–101 for the importance of
monument and temple construction amidst the tombs outside the Porta
Capena. The area outside the Porta Capena remained an important area for
elite competition to the reign of the Emperor Augustus who named the area
Regio 1 in his reorganisation of the city and beyond to subsequent emperors
Trajan, Lucius Verus, Septimius Severus, and Caracalla.

48 See Coarelli (2007) 433 ff. for extant monuments beyond the Milvian Bridge.

49 Lanciani (1892) 276.
50 Lanciani (1892) 284.
51 See Horace *Satires* 1.8, 7–16 for the conversion of necropolis into gardens.
52 The bibliography for the Tomb of the Scipios is extensive. For a recent analysis of the various stages of construction and the placement of the sarcophagi, see Coarelli (2007) 367–362.
53 See Coarelli (2007) 373–374 and Toynbee (1971) 113–118.
54 See Coarelli (2007) 404 ff. for tombs along Via Latina.
55 For tombs along the Via Appia, see Coarelli (2007) 365–400 and Ivana Della Portella, ed., *The Appian Way: From Its Foundations to the Middle Ages* (Los Angeles, 2004).
56 Statius *Silvae* 5.1.222–246 describes the tomb in a highly allusive epic ekphrasis narrative that evokes the same mythological Vergilian landscape used to describe his father's tomb in *Silvae* 5.3.
57 For the transition of pagan and Christian burials, see Lucrezia Spera, 'The Christianization of Space along the Via Appia: Changing Landscape in the Suburbs of Rome' *American Journal of Archaeology* 107.1 (2003) 23–43.
58 See Coarelli (2007) 442.
59 For tombs along the Via Aurelia, see Coarelli (2007) 438–439.
60 See Lanciani (1892) 269 ff. for the necropolis at Doria Pamphilj with columbaria behind the Casino (c. 1660) that resembled those along the Via Latina.
61 A necropolis along a stretch of an ancient Roman road (identified as Via Triumphalis) was discovered during the construction of the Vatican autopark for the Jubilee. See Bodel in Brink and Green, eds (2008) 178 with recent bibliography and Coarelli (2007) 359.
62 For tombs in the St. Peter's Necropolis, see Coarelli (2007) 354–359 and Toynbee 138 ff.
63 The historian Suetonius, however, makes the extraordinary claim that some survivors of the Great Fire in 64 CE sought shelter in tombs (*Life of Nero*, 38.2), thus turning tombs into temporary homes that the living shared with the dead. Contemporary Japanese "corpse hotels" for those awaiting cremation extend the housing metaphor. See "Japan's death industry reaps grim profits" *Reuters* 12 September 2011. For the 'houses' of the dead, see Andrew Wallace-Hadrill in Brink and Green, eds (2008) 39–77, Bodel in Brink and Green, eds (2008) 190–195 for his cautioning that Romans did not arrange themselves in death as they did in life, Regina Gee 'From Corpse to Ancestor: The Role of Tombside Dining in the Transformation of the Body in Ancient Rome' Fredrik Fahlander and Terje Oestigaard (eds) *The Materiality of Death: Bodies, Burials, Beliefs. BAR International Series* 1768 (2008) 59–68, and Valerie M. Hope, 'A Roof over the Dead: Communal Tombs and Family Structure' in Ray Laurence and Andrew Wallace-Hadrill (eds) *Domestic Space in the Roman World: Pompeii and Beyond. Journal of Roman Archaeology* (Portsmouth, RI, 1997) 69–88.
64 In the case of Gaius Munatius Faustus, he is commemorated in both locations: his cremated remains were placed in a simple memorial outside the Nucerian Gate but his wife Naevoleia Tyche built a more impressive cenotaph memorial to him outside the Herculaneum Gate in the form of a tower

with a full inscription and scene displaying her husband's generosity.

65 See Lanciani (1901) 91–98 for the systematic destruction of roadside tombs.

66 See Lanciani (1901) 209–210 for the monuments that were spoliated: 250 large marble blocks were taken from the tombs of the chariotter Aelius Gutta Calpurnianus; of Lucius Nonius Asprenas, consul 6 CE; of Valerius Nicias; of a patrician lady named Postuma, and from an unknown tomb of pyramidal shape which stood on site of present day S.M. dei Miracoli in Piazza del Popolo.

67 A column erected opposite the Basilica of S. Sebastiano ad Catacumbas also commemorates the restoration.

68 Pius IX selected the Basilica of S. Lorenzo fuori le Mura for his burial, rather than St. Peter's or even S. Sebastiano ad Catacumbas. His choice fits his efforts in inserting his legacy into the urban and Christian fabric of Rome in as many high visibility places as possible. His numerous inscriptions all over the city advertise his urban renewal efforts and his patronage and restoration of antiquities. Ironically, for a Pope who knew the value of processions, a mob tried to dump his coffin into the Tiber when his body was ceremoniously moved from St. Peter's to S. Lorenzo fuori le Mura on 31 July 1881.

69 For contemporary British artists at Rome, see Michael J. H. Liversidge and Catharine Edwards (eds) *Imagining Rome: British artists and Rome in the Nineteenth Century* (London, 1996).

70 See Lanciani (1901) 178, 210.

71 For a survey, see Erwin Panofsky, *Tomb Sculpture: Four Lectures on Its Changing Aspects from Ancient Egypt to Bernini* (New York, 1964).

72 Braci's monument combines elements from Bernini's tomb designs and is roughly contemporaneous with two other pyramid tomb designs by Bernardino Ludovisi for Cardinal Giorgio Spinola in S. Salvatore alle Coppelle (1744) and by Ferdinando Fuga for Alessandro Gregorio Capponi in S. Giovanni dei Fiorentini (1746) that feature portraits of the deceased in an oval medallion against a pyramid.

73 The Neoclassical funerary monument to Clelia Severini (1825) by Pietro Tenerani in S. Lorenzo in Lucina, Rome is less restrained: the relief depicts a woman removing her veil as she departs from her husband who is seated with downcast head with his hand in hers. A dog on hind legs looks up at the woman as an allegory of grief sits facing the scene with hair unbound, robe dishevelled, and hands clasped at her face. The visible signs of grief displayed by the allegory contrasts with the calm expressions on the couple's faces.

Chapter IV

1 Quote from MSNBC.com by Michael Rubinkam, 'Widow lived with corpses of husband, twin.' *Associated Press* 5 July 2010.

2 'The Shrine Down the Hall' *The New York Times Magazine* 18 March 2010. See also, Joanna Wojtkowiak and Eric Venbrux 'Private Spaces for the Dead: Remembrance and Continuing Relationships at Home Memorials in the Netherlands' in Maddrell and Sidaway (2010) 207– 221.

3   See George E. Dickinson and Heath C. Hoffmann, 'Roadside memorial policies in the United States' in *Mortality* 15.2 (2010) 154–167.

4   On the loss of his wife's outgoing message that he had replayed every day since her death three years previously, Charles Whiting explained, 'That's the only recording of her voice that I have,' Whiting told The Journal News. 'Every time I listened to my messages, I heard her voice saying, 'This is Catherine Whiting.' It was like she was still with me when I heard that. Now they took her voice away.' Quotation from 'New York Man Loses Dead Wife's Voice Message in Phone Service Upgrade' *The Associated Press* 17 March 2008.

5   Pliny, *Letters* 6.10.6: *Nam cui non est verendum, quod videmus accidisse Verginio? cuius iniuriam ut indigniorem, sic etiam notiorem ipsius claritas facit.* Cited is the text of Betty Radice, *Pliny: Letters and Panegyricus* (Cambridge and London, 1972) 416.

6   Compare the epitaph that Thomas Jefferson wrote for himself that does not mention his presidency among life accomplishments.

7   For other examples, see Robert Wyatt, 'Art as Afterlife: Posthumous Self-Presentation by Eminent Painters' in Mitchell (2007) 193–207.

8   Epitaphs can also identify the living. See Stanley Brandes, *Skulls to the Living, Bread to the Dead* (Malden, MA, Oxford, Victoria, 2006) chapter: 'The Poetic of Death' 93–116 for Spanish poetic epitaphs composed to the living called *calaveras* (= skulls).

9   See '"Smoking killed me" marks his hearse and grave: warning sign was dying wish of British man with emphysema.' *The Associated Press* 3 March 2010.

10 According to Humphreys (1980) 114: 'With the exception of the monuments to the very old, verse epitaphs and reliefs do not emphasize the continuity of a lineage over time; they portray the intimate relationships of the nuclear family in an idealised, timeless present. Piety to dead ancestors is not their theme. Only a few inscriptions and periboloi contradict this impression.'

11 *IG* 10650. Bibliography on Ampharete's stele is extensive, I found the following particularly helpful: S.B. Pomeroy, *Families in Classical and Hellenistic Greece. Representations and Realities* (Oxford, 1997).

12 *IG* 12, 5, 310, 3–10 from Paros, second century BCE.

13 G. Kaibel, *Epigrammata Graeca (EG)* (Berlin, 1878) 56 from Athens, pre-Roman period. See Lattimore (1962) 243.

14 *IG* 12, 1, 153, 2. From Rhodes, third century BCE.

15 *EG* 175, 3–5. Found in Athens, fourth or fifth century CE.

16 For the grouping of family tombs, see Humphreys (1980) 105–112.

17 For a detailed analysis of Latin epitaphs, see Hope (2009) 166–171; Carroll (2006) 126–179, Erasmo (2008) 159–180 and Arthur J. Pomeroy, *The Appropriate Comment* (Frankfurt am Main, Bern, New York and Paris, 1991) 'Roman Death Notices' 110–125.

18 *Corpus Inscriptionum Latinarum (C.I.L.)* I, 2. 1368. Found in Rome.

19 *C.I.L.* I, 2. 2138. Found near Cremona, possibly early first century BCE.

20 *C.I.L.* 9.3184. From Corfinium. See E. Courtney, *Musa Lapidaria: A Selection of Latin Verse Inscriptions* (Atlanta, 1995) 166–167; 376.

21 *C.I.L.* 6.13696. Found along the Via Appia, Rome, second–first century BCE. See Courtney (1995) 38–39; 214–215.

22   See Carroll (2006) 4, 126, and 266.

23   *CE* 198. Found in Rome.

24   *CE* 653, 4. Found in Umbria (373 CE).

25   *CE* 755,1. Found in Rome.

26   The tweets of Teju Cole, the "Grim Tweeter," have attracted a cult following for the sardonic wit of his eulogies: "In all the time he was an amateur electrician in Lugbe, near Abuja, Idem Kalu, 29, touched the wrong wire only once." Another: "Pauline Rivera, 20, repeatedly stabbed, with a hatpin, the face of the inconstant Luthier, a dishwasher of Chatou, who had underestimated her." The digital footprint of the dead is increasingly becoming a legacy and an issue to survivors concerned with online safety and privacy. See Rob Walker, 'Cyberspace When You're Dead' *The New York Times* 9 January 2011.

27   The companion website www.themourningpost.com allows visitors to create or search for a memorial.

28   For the history and tour locations of the Quilt, visit the official website: www.aidsquilt.org.

29   Jonathan Woods, 'NYC murals pay tribute to victims of 9/11 attacks' *Photoblog: Conversations Sparked by Photojournalism on MSNBC.com Photoblog* 4 August 2011 with images by Reuters photographer Shannon Stapleton. Sometimes the traffic signs convey the images of death. Digital signs that first display the outline of a pedestrian change to a skeleton crossing the street to warn motorists of the dangers of exceeding the speed limit. See Michael M. Grynbaum, 'A Spooky Reminder to Obey the Speed Limit' *The New York Times* 12 May 2011.

30   Keith Goetzman, 'Ghost Bikes for Dead Riders Run Afoul of Law' *Utne Reader* 21 March 2011. See also, Leonie Kellaher and Ken Warpole, 'Bring the Dead Back Home: Urban Public Spaces as Sites for New Patterns of Mourning and Memorialisation' in Maddrell and Sidaway (2010) 161–180.

31   Erin France, 'Mobile Memorial Makes its Way to Greensboro' *The Athens Banner Herald* 11 April 2011.

32   Dr. John Troyer's website deathreferencedesk.org contains information on his lecture 'Morbid Ink: Field Notes on the Human Memorial Tattoo' and discussion threads on topics such as the use of cremains in memorial tattoos.

33   A testimonial by Jessica Canada posted on www.memorials.com 3 May 2010: 'My father passed away unexpectedly at a very young age, 60, by a massive heart attack. I am 31 years old and was very close with him. I wanted to have something that I could always keep very close to me, and I was with him. This necklace was more than I ever expected and prettier than what was in the picture. I purchased 2 of them, 1 for myself and 1 for my sister. [...] I know it will never bring him back, but he will always be with me from this day forward. This past weekend was my birthday and I received the necklace yesterday. It was the last birthday present that I received from him and it means so much to me[. . .]'

34   For a full discusson of the metaphor and case studies involving the relationship between the home and the cemetery, see Doris Francis, Leonie Kellaher, and Georgina Neophytou, *The Secret Garden* (Oxford, New York, 2005), 'The Grave as Home and Garden' 81–104.

35 For metaphorical routes and roots from the home garden to the cemetery, see Francis, Kellaher, and Neophytou (2005) 85: 'Many Greek study participants at New Southgate, as well as at CLCC, cultivated their home gardens to grow flowers and plants full of memories, meaning and emotional symbolism. Grave offerings created from these flowers were perceived as more special than those bought from florists: 'The roses and carnations on the grave I have grown especially for her from seedlings.'

36 See Garland (2001) 113. The war dead received special meals: first fruits (*aparchai*) were given to the Plataians who had died at Marathon (Thucydides, 3.58.4). The cult of the dead is incorporated into fifth-century BCE Athenian tragedy. Aeschylus' *Libation Bearers* centers on Electra's discovery of Orestes' libations and lock of hair at the grave of Agamemnon that becomes the site of their prayers for him to inspire Orestes to kill his mother Clytemnestra. Honeycakes are mentioned in Aristophanes' *Lysistrata* (line 601).

37 See Humphreys (1980) 100–101 for the festivals of the *Genesia* and *Anthesteria*.

38 Funerary art supplements the literary evidence for ancient ritual but it also shares the same limitations as evidence for actual funerary practices. Ian Morris, *Burial and Ancient Society: The rise of the Greek city-state* (Cambridge, 1987), 36 provides a valuable caveat when assessing physical evidence for ritual and social behaviour: 'While it is possible to make these generalisations about ritual forms, we must not lose sight of the fact that archaeologists excavate burials and not whole funerals. Archeological remains of course provide at best but a pale shadow of past funerary activity. The differences in rites dictated by the different social identities attributed to the deceased have great potential for entering the archaeological record through their material expression, though the extent to which this happens in practice depends on the particular forms the symbolism takes, and is largely culture specific. ' See also Morris' Chapter III: 'The social dimensions of early Greek Burial.'

39 Humphreys (1980) 100 argues that aristocrats could advertise their lineage through 'loud' representations of funerals on vases.

40 See Kurtz and Boardman (1971) 104; 'By far the greatest proportion of the *lekythoi* with funerary iconography show visits to the tomb. Men, women, and children come to the grave bearing tokens of remembrance – vases, garlands, and fillets with which they decorate the tomb. Some sit by the grave, mourning their loss, some fall to the ground and express their grief more openly, and others stand by quietly, occasionally covering their faces to conceal their sorrow.' Margaret Alexiou, *The Ritual Lament in Greek Tradition*. Second Edition (Lanham, MD, 2002), 7: 'The scene at the tomb is frequently depicted on vase-paintings, especially on Athenian white-ground lekythoi, and towards the middle of the fifth century it becomes more common than the scenes of prothesis and ekphora.' Most recently, John H. Oakley, *Picturing Death in Classical Athens. The Evidence of the White Lekythoi* (Cambridge, 2004) for an extensive survey of the evidence and the iconography of *prothesis* and grave visit scenes on *lekytho*i vases.

41 On the symbolism of Chinese grave meals and similarities with those of ancient Rome, see Hugh Lindsay, 'Eating with the Dead: the Roman Funerary Banquet' in Inge Nielsen and Hanne Sigismund Nielsen, eds, *Meals in a Social Context:*

Aspects of the Communal Meal in the Hellenistic and Roman World (Aarhus and Oxford, 1998) 70–71.

In Homer's *Odyssey* 11, Odysseus digs a pit to speak with the dead in the Underworld. The dead are reanimated by drinking blood offered by Odysseus: Elpenor, Tiresias, his mother Anticleia, and then 12 women. In Vergil's *Aeneid* 6, Aeneas goes to the Underworld where he meets his father Anchises who points out future (unborn) heroes.

42　Cited is the Loeb Classical Library text of A.M. Harmon, 116–117.

43　See Vermeule (1979) 58 for a relief from Thasos (c. 450 BCE) depicting dead men drinking at a banquet.

44　*CE* 838 = *CIL* 6.3257: *set si gratus homo es, misce bibe da mi.*

45　Via Laurentina Necropolis, Ostia Antica: Tomb 17–18, late first century BCE. Museo Ostiense: Inv. 10108. Found in 1937.

46　*CIL* 6.12758. See Katherine M.D. Dunbabin, *The Roman Banquet: Images of Conviviality* (Cambridge, 2003) 'Kline Monuments' 110–125 for other examples of banquet scenes depicted on funerary altars.

47　Inv. 9538/9539 c. 210 CE. See Dunbabin (2003) 120–122 for a discussion of the sarcophagus. For a parallel ritual of the serving of food to the seated dead among the Berawan of northern Borneo, see Peter Metcalf and Richard Huntington, *Celebrations of Death: The Anthropology of Mortuary Ritual* (Cambridge, 1991) 85–97. In the case of Berawan ritual, however, the feeding is literal: after placing a cigarette in the mouth of the deceased, rice is forced into their mouths. Afterwards, to signify a symbolic meal, food is placed on a plate that is hung around the neck of the deceased.

48　On meals with the dead, see Gee (2008) 59–68, E.-J. Graham 2005. 'Dining *al fresco* with the living and the dead in Roman Italy' in Maureen Carroll, D.M. Hadley, and Hugh Willmott, eds, *Consuming Passions: Dining from Antiquity to the Eighteenth Century.* (Stroud, 2005) 58; E.-J. Graham 'The Quick and the Dead in the Extra-Urban Landscape: the Roman Cemetery at Ostia/Portus as a Lived Environment' in James Bruhn, Ben Croxford and Dimitris Grigoropoulos, eds, *TRAC 2004: Proceedings of the Fourteenth Annual Theoretical Roman Archaeology Conference* (Durham 2004) 135; Dunbabin (2003) 125–140; Joan P. Alcock, 'The Funerary Meal in the Cult of the Dead in Classical Roman Religion' in *The Meal: Proceedings of the Oxford Symposium on Food and Cookery* (2001) 31–41; and Lindsay (1998) 75.

49　See Festus-Paulus 377L and Lindsay (1998) 72.

50　See Lindsay (1998) 73.

51　See Lanciani (1892) 49 ff. Compare with the Southern US custom of wearing a rose to church on Mother's Day – red if one's mother is alive or white if dead.

52　On the hungry and thirsty dead, see Alcock (2001) 36–39 and Carroll (2006) 60 for pipes at the grave.

53　See Hope (2007) 70 for the costs the dead were willing to pay for their immortality: 'Whatever the nature of his or her bequests, the testator was trying to strike a bargain with the living; money, property and philanthropic gestures could buy memory preservation and a sense of immortality.'

54　See Erasmo (2008) 185–194.

55　For a discussion of the tomb and frescoes, see Dunbabin (2003) 128–130.

56 For recent analyses of the composition and features of funeral clubs, see Hope (2009) 68–69 and Carroll (2006) 44–48. On the Lanuvian funeral club, see Lindsay (1998) 76–77. Lanciani (1892) 41 ff discusses the *sodalium serrensium* (the corporation of citizens of Serrae). Communal burial in Funeral Society tombs were common in older North American cemeteries such as St. Louis Cemetery No. 1 and Lafayette Cemetery No. 1 in New Orleans, LA.

57 For evidence for cult activities at tombs in Rome, see Carroll (2006), 42 for second century CE house tombs on the Via Latina outside Rome with *triclinia* and dining rooms for funeral feasts and 71 for evidence of cooking facilities at the Via Salaria cemetery. See J.M.C. Toynbee and J.B. Ward-Perkins, *The Shrine of St. Peter and the Vatican Excavations* (London, 1956) 61 for drainage holes in the mosaic floor of a tomb in the Vatican Necropolis.

58 At Pompeii, see for example the *triclinium* tomb of Gnaeus Vibrius Saturninus. Banqueting at tombs reflects banqueting in the home: outdoor biclinia and triclinia was common in Pompeii (often with water features) for al fresco dining (in addition to interior dining in the formal dining room or *triclinium*): House of Octavius Quartius (*biclinia*); House of Loreius Tiburtinus (*biclinia*); House of Julia Felix (Rooms 9 and 83); House of Menander (*triclinia*).

59 The number of tombs with funeral couches is impressive: Biclinia flanked the entrances to Tomb 15 (Tombs 13 and 14 that were built together with Tomb 15 also had biclinia); the nearby Tomb 16 had a fresco of a funeral meal; Tomb 29 (belonging to Veria Zosima but her inscription slab is now attached to Tomb 15); Tomb 31; Tomb 55 (with table); Tomb 69 (with table); See Fig. 16 for Tomb 77; Tomb 78; Tomb 79; Tomb 80 (with a square brick base for a table); Tomb 81. Triclinia were built at the entrances to Tomb 87; Tomb 88 (bench in front); and Tomb 90.

60 The film 'Weekend at Bernie's' based its humour on a variation of the Irish Wake by having a corpse attend a party with guests who did not know that he was dead.

61 Robin M. Jensen, 'Dining with the Dead: From the *Mensa* to the Altar in Christian Late Antiquity' in Brink and Green, eds, (2008) 107–143 examines Roman tombs as social spaces for the sharing of meals with the dead.

62 E.J. Graham (2004) 140 lists potential logistical problems: 'Interestingly, the practicality of using these dining areas for feasting may have been severely limited by their proximity to one another. The dining couches are often placed directly adjacent to, and sometimes even superimposed upon, those of the neighbouring tomb. During major festivals when these structures were presumably in use at the same time, the area would have become particularly crowded, and the diners may have been forced to recline virtually on top of one another. This apparent inconvenience indicates that practical concerns were considered far less important than the visible presence of dining facilities outside a monumental tomb and the information concerning their identity that they were capable of communicating.'

63 *CIL* I,2.2138 = 6.9583. Found in Rome.

64 (*CIL* 13.5708, 1–15 = *ILS* 8379). The translation is by Valerie M. Hope, *Death in Ancient Rome: A Sourcebook* (London and New York, 2007) 66–67.

65   Compare Tacitus' description of Petronius' suicide while dining (*Annals* 16.18–19). See Edwards (2007) 158–159 and 176–178.

66   See Mary Beard, *The Roman Triumph* (Cambridge and London, 2007) 257– 263 for the confusion in the ancient source surrounding Domitian's triumphal celebrations and Edwards (2007) 161–164 for the narrative as an anticipation of *parentalia*.

67   The integration of the dead is a feature of Brazilian literature. See Robert H. Moser, *The Carnivalesque Defunto: Death and the Dead in Modern Brazilian Literature* (Athens, OH, 2008).

68   In Bolivia, the *Dia de los Natitas* ("Day of the Skulls") festival includes the decoration of skulls (that may be in homes) with flowers and hats. For the origins and features of Day of the Dead celebrations and their growing popularity in the US, see Rigina M. Marchi, *Day of the Dead in the USA: The Migration and Transformation of a Cultural Phenomenon* (New Brunswick, NJ and London, 2009); Stanley Brandes, *Skulls to the Living, Bread to the Dead* (London, 2006); Elizabeth Carmichael and Chloë Sayer, *The Skeleton at the Feast: The Day of the Dead in Mexico* (Austin, 1991) and E.C. Vansittart, 'All Souls' Day in Italy' in *The Antiquary* (London) 1971 36: 326–330.

69   See Brandes (2006) 'The Day of the Dead and Halloween' 117–129 for a discussion of the threat posed by the commercialism of Halloween on Day of the Dead celebrations.

70   For the visiting of tombs on the Grand Tour, see Chloe Chard, 'Grand and Ghostly Tours: The Topography of Memory' Eighteenth-Century Studies 31.1 (1997) 101–108. For dark tourism, see J. John Lennon and Margaret Mitchell, 'Dark Tourism: The Role of Sites of Death in Tourism' in Mitchell (2007) 167–178.

71   Monuments are also the source and inspiration for other art: the funerary monument on the album cover of Joy Division's *Closer*, for example, was taken from Staglieno Cemetery.

72   See Erasmo (2008) 152–153 for Augustus' visit and his remark when asked whether he wanted to see the tomb of the Ptolemies that he wished to see a king and not corpses.

73   Herodian *History* 4.8.9. Caracalla's inspection of Alexander's body is cited in an anonymous fourth century CE source.

74   For the popularity of Vergil's tomb, see Melissa Calaresu, 'Looking for Virgil's Tomb: The End of the Grand Tour and the Cosmopolitan Ideal in Europe' Jas' Elsner and Joan-Pau Rubiés (eds) *Voyages and Visions: Towards a Cultural History of Travel* (London, 1999) 138–161 and J.B. Trapp, 'The Grave of Vergil' *Journal of the Warburg and Courtauld Institutes* 47 (1984) 1–31.

75   Pliny, *Letters* 3.7.10. See Erasmo (2008) 151–153 to contrast the poet Statius' visit to Vergil's grave that was motivated by literary emulation.

76   In the US, the National Museum of Funeral History, Houston, TX is the sole museum devoted to funerary culture following the closure of The Museum of Funeral Customs, Springfield, IL closed due to poor attendance. In Europe, funeral museums are located in London, Vienna, and Budapest and other cities.

77 Exhibitions such as 'Bodies...The Exhibition' display corpses in non-funerary contexts.

78 As for example, visits to Catholic churches to see the embalmed bodies of saints, popes, and other figures displayed in a glass case beneath an altar or to Capucin crypts to see mummified corpses that often displayed in various positions or with bones arranged in artistic configurations. See Antonio Fornaciari, Valentina Giuffra, and Francesco Pezzini, 'Secondary burial and mummification practices in the Kingdom of the two Sicilies' *Mortality* 15.3 (2010) 223–249 for secondary burial practices and mummification and the display of corpses in Southern Italian churches. The Museo Galileo in Florence displays the middle finger of Galileo.

79 For a discussion of contemporary accounts, see Lanciani (1892) 294–301. Compare the discovery in 1999 of a sarcophagus containing the remains of Roman woman in Spitalfields, London.

80 See Lanciani (1892) 294–301 for the citation and translation of these accounts.

81 See Suzanne Glover Lindsay, 'Mummies and Tombs: Turenne, Napoléon, and Death Ritual' *The Art Bulletin* 82.3 (2000) 476–502 for the historical and philosophical contexts in which Turenne's mummy survived and symbolized France's various political upheavals.

82 The tomb is in the form of a pyramid and depicts an assisted death scene.

83 Maria Cheng, 'Scientists identify head of France's King Henri IV' *The Associated Press* 14 December 2010.

84 See Claire Mazel, *La Mort et l'éclat: Monuments funéraires parisiens du Grand Siècle* (Rennes, 2009), Francis Haskell, *History And Its Images* (New Haven and London, 1993) 'The Musée des Monuments Français' 236–252, Christopher M. Greene, 'Alexandre Lenoir and the Musée des monument français during the French Revolution' *French Historical Studies* 12.2 (1981) 200–222 and Russell Sturgis, *A Dictionary of Architecture and Building: Biographical, Historical and Descriptive* (London, 1905) 739 entry on Lenoir.

85 See Erasmo (2008) for a discussion of the Flavian Woman as a museum piece amidst famous non-funereal sculpture such as the Capitoline Venus.

86 Frank Eltman, '9/11 Memorial: Kin Decry Plans to House Remains at Museum' *The Huffington Post* 4 April 2011.

87 For the algorithm used to group names on the memorial through 'meaningful adjacencies', see David W. Dunlap, 'Constructing a Story, with 2,982 Names' *The New York Times*. 4 May 2011.

88 Caroline Alexander, 'Out of Context' *The New York Times: The Opinion Pages*. 7 April 2011. A translation of the same Vergil quote appears on the Valiants Memorial in Ottawa, Canada in Confederation Square adjacent to the National War Monument. Nine busts and five statues commemorate key figures in Canada's military history. The Monument was dedicated by Governor General Michaëlle Jean on 5 November 2006.

PICTURE CREDITS

All images other than Figures 2, 12 and 18 are photographed and supplied by the author.

2. Terracotta Krater. Photograph © Joel Allen.
12. Stele of Megakles. Photograph © Joel Allen.
18. John Linton Chapman, 'Via Appia' 1867. Georgia Museum of Art, University of Georgia; gift of the West Foundation Collection, in honour of William Underwood Eiland. Photograph © Georgia Museum of Art.

INDEX